An Olson-Melville Sourcebook

Volume I
The New Found Land

North America

Editor: Richard Grossinger

Io/22

An Olson-Melville Sourcebook (Volume I): The New Found Land
    (North America)
Copyright © 1976 by Richard Grossinger

ISBN 0-913028-33-9

Publisher's Address:

North Atlantic Books
Route 2, Box 135
Creamery Road
Plainfield, Vermont 05567

Principal Distributor:

Book People
2940 Seventh Street
Berkeley, California 94710

This first volume of the Olson-Melville Sourcebooks is entitled "The New
Found Land," or "North America". It is issue #22 of the journal, Io. The
second sourcebook, Io/#23, is entitled "The Mediterranean," or "Eurasia".

The text was set in 10 point California by Barrett Watten at The West Coast
Print Center, Inc., Berkeley, Calif.

This project is partially supported by a grant from the National Endowment
for the Arts in Washington, D.C., a federal agency, through the Coordina-
ting Council of Literary Magazines in New York, New York.

An Olson-Melville Sourcebook (Volume I)

The New Found Land
(or North America)

Robert Bertholf: On Olson, His Melville 5
Siri Tuttle: The Stopping of The Battle 37
Richard Grossinger: The Four Badlands 48
View of Jupiter with Shadow of Io from Pioneer 10. 64
Mariner 10 Photos of Mercury, March 29, 1974 65
Mosaics of Mariner 10 Photos of Mercury, March 29, 1974 67
Robin Ridington: Eye on The Wheel 69
Russell Gregory: For a Sacred Bundle 83
James Bogan: Ptolemy Meets the Pharaoh 86
Ishmael Reed: from Flight to Canada 89
Richard Grossinger: Melville's Whale (A Brief Guide to the Text) 97
Donald F. Wellman: The Pool, The Heath-Stepper, The Wait 153
John Thorpe: Poems 157
Richard Grossinger: Three Notes on Charles Olson 165

Robert Bertholf

On Olson, His Melville

I

When Whitehead wrote, "Thus the notion of existence involves the notion of an environment of existence and of types of existences. Any one existence involves the notion of other existences, connected with it and yet beyond it," he defined a first principle of Olson's poetics.[1] The poet himself, as an object, is involved in an environment of objects and meaning, and he must consider himself in relationship with his surroundings, as a participant in a field of action which exists in a multiplicity of dependent inter-relationships with the factors in that environment.[2] "But if he stays inside himself," Olson tells us, "if he is contained within his nature as he is participant in the larger force, he will be able to listen, and his hearing through himself will give him secrets objects share (HU 60). On the other hand, if "man chooses to treat external reality any differently than as part of his own process" (HU 11) then he erects a partition between the subject and the object of perception. In separation, a hero is one who most successfully asserts his will over reality, and the slave the one least adept in that activity. The imperative of "the Lordship over nature" (CMI 13) widens the estrangement between man and his environment, isolating him from the roots of his existence, and necessitating the manufactory of catalogues and systems of thought and analysis to replace the natural, multiphasic environment, now neglected. In one lineage, modern man inherited the Judeo-Christian tradition which drove the divine out of nature, sanctioned by the biblical decree that man shall have dominion over all nature and all nature's creatures. Spirit was removed from object and fact. Though the man-made and the heroic were always secondary to the divine-made and the Son, the requirements of the systems and catalogues of symbols and analogues to attract the power of the exiled divine reigned. Olson saw this break between the spirit (energy) and the immediate object as the major fracture of meaning confronting the modern poet. In the religious community, spirit became transcendent and was denied an image; in the poetic community, language became metaphorical and symbolical, and lost the force of immediate facticity. Words lost their etymological roots in societal repetitions and became a description of an event not an enactment (Pound would say "presentation") of the event itself. Man-made systems of language and logic became enemies of the primal force, which should be conceived of as the emergence of the energy of nature coincident with, not sequestered from the life-flow which gives existence to form—the reaction of energy into morphology as a generative act.

Olson's statement of this disjunction between the sounds of words and the objects of the sounds' identification is not front page news at this late date. Driving words back to their root meanings, by clearing away the accumulation of distorting connotations, and then letting them stand forth containing within themselves primary value in a state of fact has occupied many poets of this century. Whether the condition is called "the iron dealt cleavage" (Hart Crane), "that kind of blockage exiling one's self from one's self" (W.C. Williams), "a dissociation of sensibility" (T.S. Eliot), the difference between the exact language of Cavalcanti and the decorative conceits of Petrarch (Ezra Pound), or the difference between the thing and the idea of the thing (Wallace Stevens), the message remains roughly the same. Language has lost its immediacy and vigor as a medium of expression. The procedures for correction are also similar. Each poet reached back to a past, whether actual or imagined, in which image and idea, object and sign agreed, and attempted to transfer the integrity of the historical example into his own writing. Olson speaks of the Mayan glyphs: "Signs were so clearly and densely chosen that, cut in stone, they retain the power of the objects of which they are the images" (HU 7). Like the E on the stone which comes in as the corrective example in "The Kingfishers," the glyphs contain their meaning specifically, and in a literal sense become a measure of the attunement of a culture to its environment. Referring to a Sumer poem or a Mayan glyph, Olson wrote, "each of these people & their workers had forms which unfolded directly from content (sd content itself a disposition toward reality which understood man as only force in field of force containing multiple other expressions" (ML 68). The containment of the actual content is the same as the apprehension of the primal, and an integration into an arena of perception where distinctions between sign and fact dissolve because all action has been marshalled toward grasping the process which instigated sign making in the beginning. Recognizing process as the principal act does not rob the objective of its value; rather, it reduces its surface valuation and allows the objective to emerge, to become a vector, or a vertical projection of the energy of a given environment.

Olson found models for his procedures of reclamation in the words of Pound and Williams. Yet, Melville, especially in MOBY-DICK, had already laid out a map for Olson to follow in tracing, and forcing the tracing back to the roots, the evidence that lay underneath the experience of multiplicity. The Egyptian pyramids were to Melville what the Mayan glyphs—and later the Hittite language roots—were to Olson. The open expanse of the Pacific was to Melville what the open universe propounded by modern physics and geometry was to Olson. They shared a passion for Shakespeare. They also shared a sense of literary construction as dramatic act, an indigenous touch that materials of vastly different orders engaged one another because each manifested a field of action greater than itself. Different structures declared a unique form, not the failure of the structure to meet the tenets of a critical theory. Particularly, according to Olson's view, Melville's world contained within it the contrariety of primal orders, in immediacy, and was not, necessarily, a transparent symbol of another realm of spirituality. Melville, moreover, was immersed in "essential history," which, Olson claims, has been absent for two and a half millennia because the supernatural as well as the natural has been removed from it," and, he further claims, it was removed by "discourse"—logical and systematic rhetoric suppressing the action of the supernatural (in Olson's view, equal to the demonic).[3] The divine and the demonic were immediate presences for Melville. Ishmael and Maximus, fictive narrators both, deal out tales of cosmic energies (known collectively) in a charged facticity capable of uncovering the primordial activity. Melville's example established the first structure onto which Olson originated, borrowed and transplanted the principles of his poetics of form.

It does no good, therefore, to mistake the secondary developments for the first idea, as Marjorie Perloff has done. She has argued that Olson's attentions to Pound and Williams amounted to little more than high level copying, which, finally, demonstrated "Olson's central imaginative failure."[4] One could as easily delineate the sources of Sir Philip Sidney's "Defense of Poesy" in the works of Aristotle, Minturno and Scaliger to disclaim any originality, and then point out that THE ARCADIA slighted almost every principle of Sidney's criticism. The same would be an accurate judgment against the lack of originality of Wordsworth's PREFACE, and his disregard of his own criticism in such passages as the Snowdon vision in Book XIV of *The Prelude*, for example. In like manner whether the substance of "Projective Verse" derives precisely from the work of Pound and Williams is interesting only in so far as it illustrates how the essay originated a major shift in writing and thinking about poetry. In the literary tradition it would be equally egregious to forget that Sidney's work culminated a century of critical re-thinking and pointed directly to the work of Dryden and Johnson, or that Wordsworth defined an age (though Blake didn't think so) and an operation of the imagination that clarifies, in some senses, the late poetry of Wallace Stevens. Olson's derivations, in a non-pejorative sense, are important because they made articulate and actively usable non-restrictive poetic form, in the same space that Wordsworth's derivations from John Locke and David Hartley (plus rebellion) expressed, for use, a kind of poetry addressed to the particular and based in actual emotional condition, not the conventions (in a pejorative sense) of a tradition. Periodically the poetic mind must acknowledge its antecedents, and, without anxiety, declare its freedom. Olson's work had the effect of negating the critical standards of T.S. Eliot, who, reversing literary cycles, embraced with anxiety his antecedents, and sponsored a poetry of convention, a closed system wedded to tradition; and also had the effect of by-passing Eliot, Pound and Williams as historical and cultural thinkers— though retaining their useful technical approaches to poetics—and moving back to the core of the nineteenth century experience (crossing the Great Plains) and the transformations Melville made of that fact in MOBY-DICK as a groundwork for a new poetics. Olson went to Pound and Williams to find out what was possible in verse with the enthusiasm of a convert (for he was one to poetry), to find out how to write, not to find out, fundamentally, how to think, because that process was already awakened in his affinity with Melville.[5]

Neither does it do much good to describe CALL ME ISHMAEL as a "metaphoric collage composed of various intercalated planes small and large," and to announce: "I am suggesting that, as nearly as literature can come, CALL ME ISHMAEL is the performing of a rite, and it shares with much Abstract Expressionist painting and sculpture the character of a gnosis which, as the critical receptions of CALL ME ISHMAEL indicates, attracts those who are privy to its uses and repels those who are not."[6] While it is true that typography is part of the methodology of the book, it is not all of the book, or even a major portion; and Martin Pops' introduction of the analogy with Abstract Expressionism simply adds another modification which conceals the essential affinity between Melville and Olson, and disregards the importance of the book in the growth of Olson's poetics. Ann Charters, though, does give out some specific and important information about Olson's interest in Melville; she describes the content and the features of the book, and points out the structural parallels between MOBY-DICK and CALL ME ISHMAEL. When she announces, however, "Perhaps the best approach to understanding how ISHMAEL is organized is through the shorter prose piece "Equal, That Is, to the Real Itself" (O/M 13) she betrays her procedures. By taking Olson's information about non-Euclidean geometry of 1958 as the information of 1945, she indulges an inaccuracy equalled only by her underlying assumption that, somehow, Olson's passion for Melville is exclusively divorced from his passion for poetry.

In a more schematic way, Melville's writing and Olson's writing on Melville were not uniform and continuous coefficients for either Olson's thinking or his poetry. Instead, the force of Melville's world came into Olson in two periods, and in each period Olson conceived Melville differently, and the conception had a different effect, as a factor, on the poetry.

Period I [1927-1941] Olson first read MOBY-DICK in 1927 c. when he was 17, and although the bond between the young Olson's enthusiasm for Gloucester and the sea) which were also his father's enthusiasm) and Melville must have been declared, however latently, it was not until his graduate study at Wesleyan University lead him to an M.A. thesis, "The Growth of Herman Melville, Prose Writer and Poetic Thinker" (June 1933) that the interest ripened. And as he later explained, in 1933, "It was the PIAZZA TALES that turned me on (O/M 5). So while doing graduate study at Harvard, Olson continued his work on Melville, tracking down the volumes of Melville's personal library, especially the seven volume set of the complete works of Shakespeare, and the works of Hawthorne. Under Edward Dahlberg's guidance Olson rewrote part of a paper originally written for a class taught by F.O. Matthiesson, and published it in the first issue of TWICE A YEAR (1938) under the title "Lear and Moby-Dick." From 1939-1941 Olson wrote three essays on Melville; the third, "Exodus," has a note in Olson's hand on the first page, "Start Feb 9, 1941/Adullum & Genesis done." Two of the essays, extant but not complete, "Exodus" and "Genesis," show the continued influence of Dahlberg's assumptions of a valuable humanism in Melville that must be defined and defended. The third essay, "In Adullum Lair," is now complete. There is no evidence among Olson's papers of the existence of a 400 page manuscript which Ann Charters reports was finished by 1940, read and rejected by Dahlberg as "too Hebraic, Biblical Old Testament" (O/M 9).[7]

Period II [1941-1970] From early 1941 until April 1945, Olson put aside his work on Melville in favor of employment in New York and Washington for the Foreign Language Information Service and Office of War Information. Between April and August 1945 he produced the manuscript of the present CALL ME ISHMAEL. It lacked Melville's marginalia from Owen Chase's NARRATIVE OF THE MOST EXTRAORDINARY AND DISTRESSING SHIPWRECK OF THE WHALE-SHIP ESSEX, which Olson did not procure until late fall of that year. Also between 1941 and 1945 Olson rejected, almost completely, the influence of Dahlberg's weary moralizing, as well as the idiosyncracies and indirections of his prose style. He arrived at his own view of American literature and a distinctive style marked, chiefly, by straight-forward declaration. Earlier (in 1939), Olson had read Freud's MOSES AND MONOTHEISM. And about this time, I would guess, Olson fully realized the impact of Shakespeare's plays, and Shakespeare's membership in the devil's party, on Melville, and so on this own natural affinities for Shakespeare's dramatic techniques, and his vision. Freud and Shakespeare provided the impetus which allowed Olson to transform the long-familiar materials on Melville into CALL ME ISHMAEL. Certainly the book is an enactment of a perspective and methodology. But within the process of forming the enactment, Olson (with the ubiquity of Melville in him, and Shakespeare and Freud's leads) was transformed into a poetic thinker. While the notion of a field of action derives basically from modern physics—as does the notion of poetry as energy (Heisenberg's quanta)—in MOBY-DICK Melville displayed the Pacific as space, a field of action, a massive stage. With penetration into the primordial realms, Melville had caught, in Olson's view, the central American experience of seeking out the expanse of space in exploration, and exploiting nature for profit and gain. In the creation of the heroic Ahab possessed by the supernatural, Melville transformed the techniques of Shakespearean drama into a multiphasic form for the novel capable of containing great diversity of information. And Olson took over these features, complete with a fictive narrator, as the groundwork for a new poetics.

The second period also includes the three reviews of Melville scholarship, "David Young, David Old," "The Material and Weights of Herman Melville," and "Equal, That Is, To The Real Itself." The essays are important additions to Olson's thinking about Melville because in them he explores new ways of approaching Melville's novels. In the last two essays, Olson shows that his studies with Hans Rademacher at Black Mountain College brought major shifts in his view. Borrowing principles from non-Euclidean geometry and using notions from modern physics, Olson showed that when he came upon new information, he went back to the familiar matter of Melville and then projected that material into his poetics. And his poetics matured too during this period. He published his first main statement in "Projective Verse". He moved out from his frequent visits to Ezra Pound at St. Elizabeth's to become a close poetic friend of Robert Creeley, and an instructor for Cid Corman, as he began ORIGIN. In 1947 Olson began the project of THE MAXIMUS POEMS, and in 1951 published the poem "Letter for Melville, 1951."

II

Period I

To write MOBY-DICK Melville made himself an authority on whales and whaling: to write about Melville Olson ransacked all known sources about his subject and presented the facts as a means of bringing forth the historical immediacy of the novels. He was a thorough scholar, but he was not an explicator. As Melville dug up the documents of the whales, sought out the specifications of whaling procedures as a verification for his own experiences on the "Acushnet" (1841-42), examined the lore and mystery of the Leviathan, so Olson dug out the details of Melville's biography, attended closely to Melville's reading in preparation for each novel and displayed the strategies of Melville's development as a stylist and thinker. Both writers were scholars of the imagination. Both cultivated the imperative to inject into the work hordes of information which direct the whole plan of composition; and in the plan of composition to expose the possibilities of form as a network of internal tensions capable of containing that information. In this too an audacity exists as a judgment of concern. One of the principles of literary history deals with the ways authors take on their antecedents as examples and foundations, as Chaucer, Shakespeare and Pound took on Ovid; Blake, Milton and Dante; Eliot and Joyce, Dante. Olson took on Melville, and later Shakespeare and Dante, too. It is not that the source materials exist as the only guide, but in the great literary testaments other writers read out their own vision clearly and accurately, realizing the primary agency of the imagination as a shared force which relinquishes the past into the continuous present of the imaginative act. It is not so much a matter of direct influence as a matter of one writer confirming his imagination in the imagination of another writer; it is a matter of confirmation as a fact of the existence of the primordial world, not as a religious or psychological speculation. So, close to the concern here, Olson sought out in Melville's manipulation of information and form a foundation for his views, which were not only his views, but part of the human inheritance. He found in Melville a profile of poetics which later in his career would emerge as the data which lay under the principles of projective verse.

Olson's M.A. Thesis, "The Growth of Herman Melville, Prose Writer and Poetic Thinker," begins the progress, in the sense that here for the first time Olson displays the disciplines of scholarship which lead in the end to the ballast for THE MAXIMUS POEMS. In 1933 Olson announced that he had prepared "the first complete bibliography of Herman Melville ever attempted" (p i) as part of the prefacing materials of the thesis. He had. And in the thesis itself, which focuses mainly on the progress of style and form in the novels up to and thru MOBY-DICK, Olson shows again his care for details, and exact information. He frequently cites long passages to get the sense or feeling of the novel, not to give close readings. For each novel he provides pertinent biographical information; for example, the descriptions of TYPEE and OMOO are preceded by accounts of Melville's adventures in the South Seas. And he supplies lists of the informing sources—what he calls Melville's documentation—for each book, noticing, when possible, Melville's reading before each book. About MARDI, for example, he writes: "It is exasperating to know so little about Melville's reading and activities for these years from January 31, 1847, to April 14, 1849, because the result, MARDI, is overwhelming" (p 49). He wants to know what went into the making of each novel more than he wants to analyze the meaning and structure, for his method is to set out the ambience of information in which the novel exists, not make up a secondary evaluation of its literary significance, allegorical or symbolical. He is more concerned with how the accuracies of Melville's style contain the unraveling of the tale.

Yet, Olson is distanced from his own discussion, as if he were testing Melville to discover what there was of value in the works that he might use, or, as if Olson were probing around to discover the principle of attraction between himself and Melville. One of the discoveries which surfaced later was the simple principle that the past was available for use in the present, and that by the process of returning to the past, to a beginning, the poet might be able to reconceive himself as reborn in the presence of the materials of first things. Just as Melville set out the features of the "mystical cosmetic" (M-D 193) of whiteness in nature as an active force which reached into the present in the climactic chase after Moby Dick, and the diabolical presence in the black mass of the harpoon which becomes part of the "the black tragedy of the melancholy ship" (M-D 485), so Olson presents for contemporary viewing the facts about John White and the Dorchester Company, in such poems as "Letter 10," "Letter 23," (MP 45, 99), "THE BE-GINNINGS (facts, June 6th 1963)" (M-IV 65, 183), or the activities of William Stevens, "The First Maximus" (M 31), in such poems as *the winning thing* (M-IV 48), or "William Stevens" and "Stevens Song" (M-3 28, 30). These facts are as present in Olson's notion of POLIS, as Melville's facts were present for his sense of the Pacific chase as a field of action.

The center of the thesis is the discussion of MOBY-DICK. In 1933 Olson was not aware (no one was) of the existence of two version of the novel; and while he knew of Melville's reading of Shakespeare (he cites the letters, fully, to Evert Duyckinck in the New York Public Library, which were then little known), as well as his friendship with Hawthorne (he cites from Melville's "Hawthorne and his Mosses"), he did not make the sharp designations of influence that would later appear in CALL ME ISHMAEL. He describes the book in comparison with Shakespeare and the Fates of Greek tragedy; and in noting the "sickle-shaped lower jaw" of the white whale mentions "the wealth of epic similes" (p 129), not the Freudian meaning of slaying the father which so directs the later discussions. He talks of Ahab: "Like Satan, he fell when passion stood upon the neck of reason. He was a Prometheus bound, bound to the massy hulk of the White Whale. He has stolen the fire of wrath from the gods and by its very strength did he perish" (p 131). In discussing the whaling chapters and their placement in the flow of the book he notes: "Like the comic plot of an Elizabethan play they serve to break the tension of Ahab's mad pursuit of the whale. They ground the book, give it a foothold in reality. They deliberately brake the movement" (p 126). There is obvious admiration for Melville's accomplishment here, especially for the way Melville achieves for the first time a combined unity of data and form. While he realizes Melville's penetration into the primordial world, this penetration does not become a mythological or psychological necessity; instead he by-passes the symbolic in favor of a discussion of the prose style, giving special praise to Melville's use of the catalogue.

Olson devotes little space to the novels (he eliminates the poetry from the study) after MOBY-DICK. Though he says that sorrow and woe dominate Melville's disposition in the final 40 years, he also recognizes a decline in the later works, in PIERRE, for example, where "Melville had again lost his feeling for sequence" (p 163), yet he places the blame on the family situation and Melville's natural melancholy, not in the pews of Christianity, as he would later. Thought, not art, grew in the later years, he announces. The study's final sentences hint at Olson's later concerns: "He was a poetic thinker and this intuition no logic could destroy. It was because of this perception that he chose as his companions from the past in ways of doubt Ishmael, Solomon, and Timon" (p 179). The thesis was a beginning, and while the charged concerns for space, which frame CALL ME ISHMAEL, do not enter here—nor does the strenuousness of betrayal as a psychological factor or the whaling industry as an economic factor—the thesis provided Olson with a basis for his further research and discovery.

****

The major literary event influencing Olson's thinking about Melville between the completion of the thesis and the publication of the essay "Lear and Moby-Dick" in 1928 was the discovery of the set of Shakespeare "in glorious great type," which Melville had read and annotated, in the possession of Mrs. Francis Osborne, a grand-daughter of Melville, in 1934. Olson was dedicated to basic research, seeking out the evidence of what went into the making of MOBY-DICK. In the thesis Olson had not emphasized the influence of Shakespeare, though he noted its place in both MARDI and MOBY-DICK, but in the 1938 article he came right up front and announced: "I propose a Melville whose masterpiece, MOBY-DICK, was actually precipitated by Shakespeare. Shakespeare's plays became a great metaphor by which Melville objectified his own original vision" (L &MD 165). Olson's proposal about the influence of Shakespeare was an original, documented headline in 1938, but now is a commonplace of scholarship. Most interesting, perhaps, for the present purpose, is Olson's announcement: "What is peculiarly clear is that after reading Shakespeare Melville found the shape in which he could make his own vision most apprehensible—MOBY-DICK. The past—and it included Shakespeare—was usable" (L&MD 172). In Melville's example Olson found a pattern that would free his imagination from history's domination. Melville's mind was not impeded by the tragic vision of Shakespeare: rather it helped Melville toward "the free articulation" (L&MD 166) of that vision. It was a means toward freedom of expression, and the utility of generating a new form as a medium and vehicle for a new vision.

Most of the article gets taken over into the Shakespeare section of CALL ME ISHMAEL, with some alteration, so is familiar. It should be noted here, however, that in the essay Olson decides that *King Lear* informs MOBY-DICK more than any other of the plays, and that Melville, like Shakespeare, was concerned with both the origins of evil and the ways the forces of blackness work in the lives of men. And while both writers were concerned with a tragic condition of man suffering, Melville produced a tragedy in a democratic stance—"a concept of democratic prose tragedy" (L&MD 188) Olson calls it. He also fully realizes the dramatic structure of the novel, and its relationship to the five act structure of an Elizabethan play, especially the careful placement of the whaling chapters (as he did in the thesis) as well as the dramatic features of characterization, soliloquies and narrative plot. Olson emphasizes the structure of the novel, and the place of the narrator, Ishmael: "Ishmael is fictive, imagined, as are Ahab, Pip and Bulkington, not so completely perhaps, for the very reason that he is so like his creator. But he is not his creator: he is a chorus through whom Ahab's tragedy is seen, by whom what is black, and what is white magic is made clear.... He is passive and detached, the observer, and thus his separate and dramatic existence is not so easily felt. Unless his choric function is recognized, however, some of the vision of the book is lost." (L&MD 177). Here in 1938 is the beginning of the voice of Maximus, who in "I, Maximus of Gloucester, to You," asserts himself as distinct from the author, though made by him,

> I, Maximus
> a metal hot from boiling water, tell you
> what is a lance, who obeys the figures of
> the present dance
>
> (M, 1)

And who at the end of that first poem attests to his position of authority as the director of the action of the poems to follow, the builder of the nest that is the polis of Gloucester:

> The nest, I say, to you, I Maximus, say
> under the hand, as I see it, over the waters
> from this place where I am, where I hear,

14

can still hear

(M, 4)

Like Ishmael, Maximus knows the facts and factors of his situation; he is the fictive narrator who creates the scene of the city, by seeing accurately, reading carefully, and imagining well. His voice is involved, yet his view is detached; because he roams freely through the historiography of Gloucester (as a place and an idea), and follows the methodology of discovering first facts, the evidence that lies under, he is the single artificer of the world in which he roams, and which he prepares for others to roam. He is the creator, and the survivor.[8]

****

Olson was still under the influence of Edward Dahlberg's moralizing when he wrote the three essays on Melville, "Exodus," "Genesis," and "In Adullam's Lair." The first sentences of the final article show that off: "Infolded lies and truths, errors and beauty is life, and its convolutions are endless. Life is not life which sees an end to itself. Death ends but my life, it assaults life not itself, thus death's endless feed on person: Carnivore Worm, frantic enemy" (IAL 1). But Olson does launch out in a new direction, and in order to have that direction straight, I will quickly give a sense of the articles.

"When the Pequod sunk," Olson tells us, "did Herman Melville" (IAL 2), a victim of his own creation, a man who feared death and had no faith in life. Melville reached his artistic apogee in MOBY-DICK, and the novels after that one show a marked decline, mainly because the white magic of a redeeming Christ entered Melville's life and replaced the presence of the supernatural, which Melville associated with the demonic. "Christ was a Dead Sea where Melville made brackish the waters of his spirit. The Pacific of him Shrunk to a Sodom Lake, bitumen and ashes.... Christ buried Melville's imagination fathoms down" (IAL 5, 6). Melville sought Christ because he lacked love: "Nor man nor woman did Melville know in love" (IAL 8); but Christ failed Melville too, a man with "the sensual in the cell of himself" (IAL 10), anxious and denied, bound in a "white marriage" (IAD 11), he became a prisoner of his own frustrations. The heroes of the later novels wither, as he says in a passage which is taken over into CALL ME ISHMAEL:

> Pierre's sight withers, his eyes "fretted with wires." Billy stammers. Melville, flawless himself, but twisted within, marks his men. The flesh refused, he had to lacerate what had, in denial, lacerated him. In THE CONFIDENCE MAN a Negro beggar crawls along the deck a cripple, a Pip befouled. None bear stigmata like Ahab's but all are flicked and

striate, even to Billy's dolled and rosied face. When the body is not what it is, it shall be what it is not. From the loosened web of Melville's desire for love arose "the soft curled hermaphroditical Christ" he sought inevitable and painful was it he should clothe the Christ of THE CONFIDENCE MAN in white doeskin—and make him a MUTE.   (IAL 13-14)

"Ahab," Olson argues, "is a pagan Faust, brother to Enceladus, and Prometheus, pre-Christian, Dionysian" (IAL 14). On the other hand Christ made Melville mute; and as he says in conclusion:

His body deprive and celibate, space burst and broken for him, Melville, alone and lacerate, wanted to unstring his chords and hear not his own voice. Dying into life he feared; instead he found in the self a death which has no life. Melville is the tragedy of the Immaculate: the White of Prime shall, in the end, alone from life, corrupt to Leper Death. The First, unbegotten, shall be the Last, and whiteness all. The Single Self is suicide of spirit and of speech. There can be no Conclusion but Nothing. No One escapes to tell the Tale.   (IAL 17)

Later Olson connected the decline with Melville's trip to the Holy Land (1856), but here he warns against the protection of Christ, who takes away the direct confrontation with evil and pain, removing mystery from the unknown, the center of the supernatural sense of MOBY-DICK. The announcement against Christ is so strong here, and the preparation for the reading of Melville's life as one of betrayal so potential, I would guess that Olson had not yet read MOSES AND MONOTHEISM, which fully informs the next essay "Genesis."

In "In Adullam's Lair" and "Genesis" Olson takes a different stance toward essay writing than in the earlier thesis and the essay "Lear and Moby-Dick," in the sense that he is now using the materials as a basis for the exposition of a thesis, not simply supplying evidence, the facts, and then offering an interpretation of the facts. "In Adullam's Lair" supplied the thesis of Melville's mythic enfeeblement caused by Christ, and "Genesis" literally proposes a genesis, a return to the primordial start and the progress forward, but with Olson's slant on origins as the determination.

In the Beginning was the White Whale. Melville was Moses, the Pacific his Pentateuch. In the birth of the world did Melville begin, and *Whiteness* was upon the face of the deep. The first Day and the Morning thereof not the First Night did Melville comprehend.[9]   (G 1, UC)

"The Fall was the Abomination of Whiteness. Adam was Sin as Spot" (G 2, UC), Olson continues, and then announces that his version of the fall took place when man intruded upon space; at that point God became an enemy, and Melville, in the realization of the Pacific as primal space, was forced into the position of a primordial contrary. He joined the powers of blackness, in rebellion:

16

> Pale to white is black, and extreme of Ancient is Satan, Lucifer's rebellion
> Melville shared, and kin to kill, intimates of failure were they.... Frustrate
> of Prime divine, profane First was alternate, and Melville located his
> Satan—and hell—upon the fields of heaven.   (G 1, UC)

With the world fractured into contraries, Melville followed the pattern of Satan, who as brother was the first "son to strike the Father archetype Enceladus, early Prometheus, elder Ahab":

> Mithra doth slay the Bull, and Zeus to become Zeus doth castrate Kronos.
> In the First Adam the Father created the Son who, once born, doth sickle
> and make sterile the Source.   (G 4, UC)

And all at once Ahab's assault on the white whale, evil, the biggest force of the Pacific space and its ruler, its natural aristocrat, takes on a Freudian modification which aligns the combat with the recurring pattern in history, myth and literature. The whale is "the monomaniac incarnation of all these malicious agencies which some deep men feel in them" (MD 181). The events and visions of the past become usable because they can be understood as later manifestations of primal acts. In Freudian terms, or in the terms set out in MOSES AND MONOTHEISM, Ahab is the exiled son, who, twice wounded in the battle with the father, the power of space and white (cf. "The Whiteness of the Whale," MD 185), willingly accepts this combat, and rejects the consolations and appeasements offered by Christ to remove the stain of the first murder of Moses—that act which spreads guilt on all mankind—and launches himself monomaniacally on the drive to participate in prime actions. He blares defiance at the divine world, breaks his instruments of navigation, and enters the battle, risks destruction in the struggle of the son against the father. In Olson's argument, when Melville contracted with Christ, he accepted his guilt for the act of murdering the father, and also accepted the salvation and redemption offered by the Christ: he chose a soothing bargain and left undone what Ahab began, the challenge of the primal world.

> Melville's ethic is mythic. His share was primary: the concord of Space,
> "sweet milk" to Macolm and to Melville, Man and his blood did curdle
> and make sour. Not acts but Act brought Melville's Guilt. Man's 'imperial'
> theme is the Fruit of First Murder, and no compass of conscience mea-
> sures it: immediately Macbeth murders he strides hugely forward into the
> mystery and leaves his still sexed Lady stunned and forgotten.... Melville
> knew no answers called Conduct. Dogs did lick his Ahab's blood, but it
> was that Canine of Ocean, Moby-Dick, who broke Ahab in its jaws and
> with salt and water, not with dust, did mix his blood, and drink.
>   (G 7-8, UC) (CMI 83)

Melville's novels turn away from the primordial battle after MOBY-DICK and concern themselves with societal matters, with incest and trickery, with the decline of man as hero who embraces Christ, until, as he said in "In Adullum's Lair," it becomes impossible for Billy to speak, in his innocence, and he must strike out physically.

Instead, Olson insists, now with the presistence of a man who has uncovered a mystery, that all men are involved in the activities that Melville uncovered. He has moved fully into Freud's world, as it was stated in THE INTERPRETATION OF DREAMS, namely that dreaming draws up the dreamer's childhood: "Behind the childhood of the individual we are then promised an insight into the phylogenetic childhood, into the evolution of the human race, of which the development of the individual is only an abridged repetition influenced by the fortuitous circumstances of life."

> Birth possesses a man of a backward behind the womb, behind conception. Bodies bear more than the harvest of behavior, either the child's or the father's. In the underground river of the blood are many children, many fathers. For the span of the body is not the beginning and the end, its birth and death rode posts.... At once am I Moses and the Author of tomorrow's Adam—or I am nothing. What is common to Adam, Melville, and a man, you, today, is human life.... Men are duplicates, repeat of organism, but that very monotony is man's majority: life reenacts itself in each.   (G 11-12, UC)

Olson has recognized that same pattern of experience Melville had found in Shakespeare, and announces it here with enthusiasm. The initiation into humanity's action, past and present, was an initiation into the realm of poetry, where all evidence gets marshalled to the uncovering of primogenesis.

> Vengeance is the fable. A man of the elements called Ahab seeks to avenge himself, Lamech, both Cain and Abel, Lucifer, seventy and seven fold upon a Monster of white, very Gorgon, named Moby-Dick. And if the true son of Adam and Eve after the murder of Abel was Seth, so was the false son of Osiris another Seth, Egyptian Cain who became the Boar and slew the God. The historical Diodorus Siculus has it that Osiris, like Ahab, was mangled, rent into fourteen pieces and scattered upon the waters of the Nile where fish ate his phallus.[10]   (G 21, UC)

Olson provided a conclusion to the essay which fully supports his entrances into the archetypal world, where Ahab enacted, as Olson, the poet, will enact, the ancient attunements:

> *Moby-Dick* is the book of Genesis of the Apocrypha, the hidden parable of man the son's love and hate for the father who is god. In Ahab's assault upon the white whale, Melville disclosed truths of the First Man even the Kabala, which tells of Lilith wife before Eve whom Adam begat nothing

but evils, dare not reveal. Melville rent a veil, man knows, to his terror, in his veins. The dark, uncanonical birth all men experience Melville allowed more light to penetrate. He counted birthdays as the Hebrews did: a son's years gathered not from the son's birth but from the father's death. Another Moses Melville wrote in *Moby-Dick* the book of the law of the Blood.   (G 29, UC)

While not completely available for reading, "Genesis" does give some indication of the turn Olson took in his views toward Melville. There is a concern for space, where man enacts his battles with the primordial, and there is an endorsement of the presence of the father/son archetype which discloses for use the literature of the past as a verification of the primal genesis as well as portents of the present. "Exodus," of which only two versions of the first page are available, offers two additional clues about the direction of Olson's thinking. Olson has come to the notion of space as the one central fact of the American experience. "Horizon," he says "enigmatically spawns space, and the malice of America is space, where man can only stride in fool's hope to diet, like the Chameleon, of the air":

> Horizon makes the earth a stage and men upon it puppets. So circumscribe no tragedy of flesh or spirit can, in old ways, be enacted.... There is no other way; confront man you cannot because he is no where; he is in motion, driven, a looped and windowed thing. Melville understood enough to raise the stage of earth above horizon and play his tragedy out against the background of what an American is committed to. Space. *Moby-Dick* is pageant, and Ahab a Job of Silhouette.... (mss breaks off)
> (E 1, UC)

The focus on the concept of space, is, of course, given more prominence in CALL ME ISHMAEL, where it frames the book by organizing the first and final sections. In another version of the first page, Olson compares Ahab's journey to *The Odyssey* and *The Divine Comedy*: "They (TYPEE, OMOO AND MARDI) are studies of another frontier discovered and explored, the South Seas, more to be compared to Parkman's Oregon Trail than to" (mss breaks off). The implication here is that Olson has begun to shift his attention away from the five part structure of the Elizabethan play that he found behind MOBY-DICK to the three part structure, which, Donald Byrd tells us,[11] became a principle of structure for THE MAXIMUS POEMS. There is also the hint that Olson is beginning to move away from Dahlberg's moral views to his own views of American literature and history asserting value and importance of their relationship with geographic factors.

Period II

CALL ME ISHMAEL is both a collect and a lens. In the book Olson brought together sections from his previous essays on Melville and combined them with an intensified awareness of Freud's fictive mythology of the son in conflict with the father, plus the guilt for the slaying of Moses, as first act, as well as the totemic cannibalistic feast which followed the slaying of the father. He also added new information and redirected old perspectives to make the book into both a statement and a demonstration of a methodology. The statement and the demonstration, further, amounted to a declaration of intention which leads to an initiation into the world of poetry, the project of THE MAXIMUS POEMS in 1947, and finally to the understructure of "Projective Verse." "Written," as Olson tells us, "at a clip" (O/M 9) between April 13 and August 6, 1945, the manuscript was added to in the fall of that year. After Pound's approval and T.S. Eliot's rejection—Eliot, of Faber and Faber, thought the book mainly for an American audience, but thought too that Olson should be encouraged in his work—the book was printed by Reynal and Hitchcock in 1947.

The contents of the book and the relationship of the parts to the structure of MOBY-DICK, for better or for worse, have already been described by Ann Charters. Instead of repeating that discussion, I would like to notice the sources of the various parts and where possible—and without being too tedious—to indicate the changes Olson made in putting the book together.

The story of the Essex, which begins the narrative, was added several days after the composition of the whole. Olson had known about Owen Chase's narrative since his M.A. Thesis, but now the story of cannibalism holds a dominate place in the enactment of the sequence of facts and presentations. Melville had described in MOBY-DICK how the whale itself provides the fuel to boil its own blubber down, and Olson in "Genesis" had explained "Cannibalism is it all" (G 21). Beside being a fact of existence, as a way of staying alive in a small boat in the Pacific Ocean, the incident has a direct connection, as a law of the blood, with the story of the "Globe"— "Fact #2"—which Olson discovered in the National Archives in 1945, and a further connection with the story of Moses in the book. All reach out from Freud's MOSES AND MONOTHEISM. According to Freud, after the brothers have slain the father, they participate in a totemic feast at which they eat the father. The communion service, he explains, re-enacts this primal act. The killing of the father, in this case the officers of the "Globe" by Samuel B. Comstock, repeats the first murder, restates it with violent simplicity. That slaying is but a version of the slaughter Ahab would carry out against the white whale, with incredibly complicated motivations, most dealing with vengeance, but some having to do with himself as a repetition of Osiris, the Egyptian, who, in the extended space of the most ancient ocean performs the act of primordial life.

The Pacific Ocean "rolls the midmost waters of the world, the Indian Ocean and Atlantic being but its arms" (MD 478) Melville writes, giving Olson a clue for his conception of space. He tells us:

> It started, for me, from a sensing of something I found myself obeying for some time before, in CALL ME ISHMAEL. It got itself put down as *space*, a factor of experience I took as of such depth, width, and intensity that, unwittingly, I insisted upon it as fact (actually tried, there, to bring it down out of the abstraction of the word of it and away from the description descriptive error of the illustrations of it I was then capable of—American geography, pre-history, and by way of the test-case, Melville, proto- or archeo-culture—by telling three sorts of stories, but setting in alongside the abstractions and the analogies three documentary narratives which I dubbed FIRST FACTS, to give space, but that noun, and those narratives the mass and motion I take it to have, the air that it is and lungs we are to live in it as our element.   (O/M 83)

In the section entitled "Call Me Ishmael," Olson sets out his proposals of space as the most important fact of the American experience, as well as the notions of the economic imperative to hold dominion over nature—"Lordship over nature"—(CMI 13) but settles mainly on the Pacific as a place of primal action, already prefigured in the great plains.[12] "It Made Noah, and Moses, contemporary to him. History was ritual and repetition when Melville's imagination was at its own proper beats." (CMI 13). Here again Olson states the conditions of archetypal action in the Pacific. Melville had recognized the morphological similarity between the ocean and the prairie, several times comparing the two, and also recognized the whale ship as a pioneer: "For many years past the whale-ship has been the pioneer in ferreting out the remotest and least known parts of the earth" (MD 107-08). While Olson does go back to "In Adullum's Lair" for the idea of Melville's "white marriage" (CMI 13), most of this section is a thorough re-vision with expansions of the original idea of space in "Exodus."

When Olson finished his manuscript in August 1945 the material from the "Usufruct" section was not included, nor was the proposition about MOBY-DICK being "two books written between February 1850 and August 1851" (CMI 35), which leads off the section "Shakespeare, or the discovery of MOBY-DICK." The material does not appear in the essays, but it does have a common source. In late August or early September 1945 Olson, while at the Harvard Library, met Howard Vincent, who was then doing research for his book on Melville, THE TRYING-OUT OF MOBY-DICK.[13] A letter from Vincent to Olson, dated 16 September 1945, indicates that the two men did have a conversation, and in that conversation Vincent told Olson that Perc Brown owned Melville's copy of Owen Chase's NARRATIVE; and that one main part of his study was the demonstration of the fact of two versions of MOBY-DICK. Vincent wrote to Olson: "I am writing to Perc Brown today asking him to hurry up on those photostats, and maybe that will get some results" (UC). A letter from Perc Brown to Olson dated 28 November 1945 tells Olson that he will let Olson see the Chase book on 30 November 1945. Olson wrote to Jay Leyda 27 January 1946 about the notes he had taken from Chase's narrative as "a recently acquired thing," and:

> The whole Essex business separates and joins Melville and myself. I come to it independently of him, and where it is the whale's act that moved him, it is the consequences to men in the open boats which, a hundred years later, catches my 20th century attention. These notes of M's go in my direction, and the curious thing is that he too was especially effected by the fate & character of Pollard. I had discovered in Nantucket what I thought was not known, that Pollard had ended as a night watch of the town. But there, in M's hand, is a pencil addition, sometime after 1851, "a night-watchman"! (UC)

The inclusion of the notes from Chase and Olson's enthusiasm over having them for his book substantiate further the place of cannibalism, or as another confirmation that the Pacific caused primal action to take place: the act itself could be seen as standing out from that space as an example of first energies which all men participate in in their time. More than another source of MOBY-DICK, Chase's NARRATIVE proved Olson's own perception of Melville as a plunger who took risks and sought prime.

In Melville's view, Shakespeare too sought prime, and Olson again confirms, following the argument of "Lear and Moby-Dick," that the reading of Shakespeare was the main cause of the formation of the novel. With two exceptions, the central sections on Shakespeare repeat the essays, in direct quotations and in revisions, so instead of repeating I will focus on the exceptions (see note).[14] While in his thesis Olson had noted that woe and sorrow were normal aspects of Melville's disposition in the last 40 years, and that he sought out fraternity with such men as Solomon and Timon, he did not emphasize the theme of betrayal as an ingredient of tragedy. Here, however, Olson writes:

> Melville took a more personal possession of the tragedy of Timon than of any of the other dark men. In *Lear* he found ingratitude, but what gave *Timon* its special intensity was that Timon was undone by friends, not daughters. (CMI 45)

In the same section Olson makes the point that "Melville had the Greek sense of men's love" (CMI 45). The betrayed hero or, "the blasted hero" Olson continues, emerges in PIERRE, where he appears as "disillusion itself, man undone by goodness" (CMI 46). And the second exception comes ringing in as a major shift in Olson's thinking about Melville:

Or recognize that our power is simply QUANTITY.
****

Or you can take an attitude, the creative vantage. See her as OBJECT in MOTION, something to be shaped, for use. It involves a first act of physics. You can observe POTENTIAL and VELOCITY separately, have to, to measure THE THING. You get approximate results. They are usable enough if you include the Uncertainty Principle, Heisenberg's law that you learn the speed at the cost of exact knowledge of the energy and the energy at the loss of the exact knowledge of the speed.   (CMI 69)

Olson is now concerned with QUANTITY, with the concept of energy motion and velocity. He has transformed the force of Melville's democratic tragedy in the geographic area of the Pacific into the field physics of Heisenberg where energy becomes the measure and not the substance, where velocity (the initiation of process) becomes more important than plot. Olson's interjection here transforms out of a Shakespeare thru Melville a notion which is coincident with modern physical theories, illustrating, I would think, the attunement between the imagination of the poet and the imagination of the physicist—each reads himself in the work of the other. So, when Olson proclaims in "Projective Verse" that he is championing "composition by field," he has the field of the multiple elements of MOBY DICK behind him. Melville's recognition of the ancient energy of the Pacific, and the enactment of that psychic and mythic energy in the diverse internally controlled form of the novel, feeds into Heisenberg's notion of quanta and Einstein's notion of fields of force. A poem is "energy" first, "A high energy-construct" (HU 52). At least one of the main principles of "Projective Verse" derives directly from Olson's study of Melville, but there is a great deal more of unspecifiable ambience which comes over into the poetry.

The essay "Genesis"—transformed—becomes the central statement of "Moses," the book of the law of the blood, and restates what Olson has called the "imperial theme," the fruit of the First murder—what Freud describes as the slaying of Moses. Cannibalism enters also as a result of the murder, yet, Olson argues Melville in MOBY-DICK understands the psychic area he had entered , and could bear the responsibility of the guilt for *the* act of slaying the father/leader, and without the comforts of Christ. He remains devoted to the Old Testament, as Father Mapple was in his sermon. Only after the trip to the Holy Land, which Olson documents with passages from Melville's JOURNALS UP THE STRAITS, and supports with passages taken over from the earlier "In Adullam's Lair," does Melville fall into the arms of Christ: "he becomes Christ's victim, and it was death, and lack of love, that let him be it" (CMI 99). "Jesus unstrung him" (CMI 104-05) Olson announces as he accounts for the declining hero of the later novels. The book comes to an end, as I mentioned above, with a discussion of Pacific man, and the notion that the movement out into the Pacific is an extension of the experience of crossing the prairies. As the citation from Dante's IN-FERNO—first used in "Exodus"—indicates, Melville thought of Ahab's as one of the three great journeys, fulfilling the grand prophecy, in a sense, of Dante's DIVINE COMEDY.

CALL ME ISHMAEL is more than an eccentric statement about Melville. Declining straight logical development, and deploying information as aspects, but not necessarily continuities of the subject of MOBY-DICK, Olson proposes to assimilate so fully the evidence, the documentation of the information that went into the novel, that his proposals become enactments of the energy of the novel and not judgments about it. "Art," Olson writes (and this extends to criticism) "does not seek to describe but to enact" (HU 10). The book enacts, then, Olson's engagement with the novel; or the material, the atmosphere of the novel becomes the ambience out of which Olson suggests a context for viewing the novel, as well as a methodology for understanding the book in terms of historical and literary movements. Olson wrote to Jay Leyda, the author of THE MELVILLE LOG, 4 February 1946:

> Maybe it amounts to this. You speak of non-interpretation, in your letter to Taylor. In other words, what you aimed at was to tell the story by documentation alone. It was precisely such documentation that I spent 13 years to assemble in order to discard. For my aim was to master such an intense interpretation that I could make the man come alive without biography. It could be that, now that we are done, the opposite can, ought perhaps to be introduced. Certainly your structure of a LOG makes the facts more engaging. And I can hope you will find my probe-prose of an order of interpretation fresh and clean.   (UC)

The collecting of documentation about Melville which began with the thesis and continued thru the essays reaches a climax here, when his methodology of criticism passed out of the order of criticism into the order of poetic disclosure. Like Melville, who entered the arena of primordial slaughter, Olson entered fully the vision of Melville and found there a grand new design which released the past for use, announced the immediate presence of the mythic world, provided a theory of exposition—composition by field—and a medium, a fictive narrator. Olson began his study of Melville as a thorough student of literature, and emerged a scholarly poet of the imagination.

* * * *

Olson's poems deal directly and indirectly with Melville. "Letter for Melville 1951" attacks the politics of the Melville Society. Olson writes about the poem in a letter to Cid Corman:

> i had the wild idea, to take the LETTER TO BE READ AWAY FROM THE CENTENARY CELEBRATION OF MELVILLE'S MOBY-DICK

24

AT WILLIAMS COLLEGE LABOR DAY WEEKEND (it was written, in a moment of flame, two weeks ago), and fire it as a bit of verse pamphleteering (something I don't know has been much done since the Elizabethans) and by god if the kids last night didn't raise the 20 bucks to have it set by electrotype in Caslon, so that we can sell it at that damned stupid celebration, and also sell it as an olson poem! [15]

Though Olson claims that Larry Hat printed the poem, Stan Vanderbeek writes that he printed the poem himself. Ed Dorn remembers working on the poem in the print shop at Black Mountain College in the summer of 1951. The poem was never sold at the Melville Conference. A single copy was delivered by special delivery to Luther Mansfield (local chairman of the conference) on Labor Day 3 September 1951, who had the task of delivering it to Eleanor Metcalf, the addressee of the letter.[16]

Olson was invited to the conference, but did not attend. In the prose section at the start of the poem he quotes from the combination announcement/advance registration form: "The Berkshire Hills are unusually pleasant at this time of year, and the conference has been timed in such a way as to avoid most of the Labor Day traffic. Those who are planning to take part in the English Institute at Columbia University on September 5-8 will find it convenient to attend both conferences." Olson uses this as the first point of scorn he heaps on the Melville Society and its members who, with several exceptions, he views as *exploiters* and *users* of Melville. Beginning with deriding comments about the food, and raising a moralistic question of whether a modern highway would have prevented Melville's fall from a cart, which later caused attacks of sciatica, Olson notes that 100 years ago Melville was already at work on PIERRE, and that the academic people have missed the time of the celebration. Melville had written that "a whaleship was my Yale College and my Harvard" (MD 110), and in the poem Olson uses this line to tell Eleanor Metcalf and her husband Henry K. Metcalf—the "Harry" of the poem—that they should not be associating with such a society. He also exempts Raymond Weaver, author of HERMAN MELVILLE, MARINER AND MYSTIC (1921), and a long time correspondent of Olson, Jay Leyda, author of THE MELVILLE LOG, as well as the "doctor" (later "the family doctor"), Henry A. Murray, who edited PIERRE (1949). But the rest of the Melville scholars do not escape Olson's "damnations" (AM 35).

Howard Vincent, author of THE TRYING-OUT OF MOBY-DICK (1949), and editor of Melville's COLLECTED POEMS' (1947) receives mighty scorn. He is the "Congregational minister's son Midwest" who put out an edition of Melville's poems with "so many carelessnesses in it that, as of this date, it is quite necessary to do it over" (AM 35). The man who will give one of the main speeches is, probably, F.O. Matthiessen, and the "one who will do the same that other did" (AM 35) is either Lewis Mumford or

Willard Thorp (Luther Mansfield suggests these names, and Howard Vincent concurs). And finally the "one very bright man" (AM 37) turns out to be Perry Miller, who delivered a lecture at the conference on "Melville and the Transcendentalists." The other references to Hart Crane and to Melville's novels and stories are explicit.

It should be remembered that in the early days of the Melville Society the atmosphere was not as polite and happy as it is today. In the 1930's there was not a great deal of interest in Melville, and those few people who were caught in his literary trap were very protective about the information they found out. Olson was familiar, in addition, with the early activities of the society. Early copies of the society's newsletter are among his papers, as are letters from Tyrus Hillway, Eleanor Metcalf, Jay Leyda, Raymond Weaver and others. I've heard the early soceity described as a group of happy vipers in fancy suits. Olson had thought that he had found THE TRUTH about Melville, even suspecting, in a metaphorical sense, "that the World would stand still" (O/M 11) when CALL ME ISHMAEL was published. It is only natural for him to attempt to protect the value he saw in Melville from others who he saw as distorting the novels for profit and advancement. Earlier Olson had written to John Woodburn, 25 October 1945:

> Weaver, Harry Murray and I have formed an unholy three against the scholars. They like none of us. They have always sniped at Weaver's book, they will give mine no break, and they have long talked down Harry Murray's minute biography to come. Maybe it's because in their own world of documents, the three of us have, successfully, scooped them.   (UC)

Feelings were intense about Melville, and the proper way of dealing with him. It might be better not to consider this poem as an indication of how mean and vindictive Olson could be, but as a testament of how much Melville was a part of his views of literature and poetic theory. After all, he came to first maturity in Melville's world.

****

Olson wrote three reviews of books on Melville, two of which are common enough discussions of the merits of the scholarship, while the third, "Equal, That Is, to the Real Itself," moves in a different direction. In "David Young, David Old" (1948), Olson praises F. Barron Freeman's edition of MELVILLE'S BILLY BUDD, because Freeman extracted from the Billy Budd manuscripts the original short story, which, under the influence of Hawthorne, Melville rewrote, and thus obscured the force of the first story. By saying that Hawthorne has an influence on Melville, Olson adds still another element that went into the making of MOBY-DICK. And, again, Olson is more interested in basic research than he is in interpretation. Picking up the lines "upon a Moebius/ materials, and the weights of pain/ and harmony" (AM 10) from "The Moebius Strip," Olson reviews Vincent and Mansfield's edition of MOBY-DICK (1952), Ronald Mason's THE SPIRIT ABOVE THE DUST (1951), and Lawrence Thompson's MELVILLE'S QUARREL WITH GOD, in an article entitled "The Materials and Weights of Herman Melville" (1952/53). In the first part of the review Olson severely debunks the work of Vincent and Mansfield, scorns the work of Thompson, but reserves some praise for Mason's discussion, admitting that the book, perhaps, could belond with the work of his favorite people—Raymond Weaver, Geoffrey Stone, Jay Leyda, Harrison Hayford and Henry A. Murray. But in the second part Olson takes off from the discussion and adds a new perspective to his view of Melville.

"Melville's importance," Olson writes,

> lies in (1) his approach to physicality, (2) his address to character as necessary human force, and (3) his application of intelligence to all phenomena as the ordering agent—what Creeley and I have elsewhere called the Single Intelligence, which is a better way of naming the total intelligence, simply that it is never more than the given man's act in the presence of *his* multiples.   (HU 112)

Olson is sponsoring a notion of the methodology of Melville, which focused a concentrated attack on the "logic and classification" as well as the idealism of the last century. "By his impeccable and continuous inquiries into what ways ideality ("transcendentalism" was the current word for it in Melville's time) no longer fit modern reality in a form proper to its content, he drove further than any of his predecessors toward forcing totality of effort to yield some principle out of itself" (HU 113). Olson is not interested in praise, but in the presentation of the physicality of reality, as he illustrates with the example of the chapter "The Tail" from MOBY-DICK, where Melville shows his "knowingness of object and motion, those factors of a thing which declare what we call its physicality (and do not mean physiology)" (HU 113). In CALL ME ISHMAEL Olson had argued that up to and thru MOBY-DICK Melville had been moving toward the containment of the concrete, and in this review he changes that to physicality, blends in the Heisenbergian principles of object and motion, and then announces: "With Melville's non-Euclidean penetrations of physical reality ignored or avoided, all the important gains he made in expressing the dimensions possible to man and to story are also washed out (HU 114). Grounding himself with the idea that Melville grasped the archaeological man and by doing it entered the mythological present (HU 115), which is a new way of saying that he sought primal reality and found it, Olson moves toward a spatialized notion of his poetic views by devaluing temporal events as repetitions in space of archaeological conditions. In MOBY-DICK, Melville was able to avoid generalizations, move beyond characterization toward "personage" with "the anti-hero Ahab" (HU 115) and make a major statement against the regulations, of whatever specifications. The Egyptian Ahab who hurled curses at the cosmos is far behind Olson at this point. The significant point here is that Olson is using the occasion of the review to expand his views about methodology—"methodology is form" (HU 114)—by stressing the importance of non-Euclidean geometry and modern physics as a means of realizing sharply just how overwhelming Melville's achievement was. The enriched view of Melville enriched also Olson's poetic theory.

The expanding and deepening continue in the review of Milton R. Stern's THE FINE HAMMERED STEEL OF HERMAN MELVILLE (1958). Olson dismissed Stern's thesis about Melville's "naturalism" as irrelevant because nineteenth century geometry, which Melville participated in without knowing it, had already redefined reality in such a way that the discussion of naturalism was at best antiquarian and at worst silly. Olson has Whitehead's PROCESS & REALITY and Herman Weyl's PHILOSOPHY OF MATHEMATICS AND NATURAL SCIENCE supporting him as he discusses the importance of MOBY-DICK as an example of a spatial designation of physicality which is an extension of actual space it describes because it, by being congruent, is an accurate measurement of the quantity, or energy, of that space. Olson quotes Melville's letter to Hawthorne: "By visible truth we mean the apprehension of the absolute condition of present things" (HU 118). And toward the end of the review he writes: "Melville wouldn't have known it to say it this way, but he was essentially incapable of either allegory or symbol for the best congruent reason: mirror and model are each figures in Euclidean space, and they are *not* congruent. They require a discontinuous jump." (HU 121). The point here is that Olson has now shifted the basis of his understanding of Melville away from the psychological, mythological and archaeological terms, to the terms of non-Euclidean geometry. The point that Melville penetrated into primordial existence now emerges as a mathematical function that makes it possible to describe the visible truth as an extension of topos, actual geography; and the projected form of the novel has a congruence with the topos, meaning that in its quantity, or its intensified arrangement, it enacts the basic deep structure of the topos. In such an arrangement the energy (previously called mythic force) contained in the physicality of the novel so confirms and projects the energy of space, presents it with such exacting immediacy, that symbols or allegory, which refer beyond their immediate structures, are no longer necessary, or even desirable.[17] At the end of the article Olson quotes from Herman Weyl but makes some adjustment in the following passage:

It is one thing if something merely retains its state until some event happens to change it—a circumstance which may occur if the subject is completely indifferent with respect to either state; it is another thing and signifies much more if the subject is not indifferent but possesses a power, an inclination as it were, to retain its state and to resist the causes of change." Hence the solution is attained as soon as we dare to *acknowledge the inertial structure as a real thing that not only exerts effects upon matter but in turn suffers such effects.* This step was taken by Riemann as early as the middle of the nineteenth century regarding the metrical structure of space; for indeed the inertial and the metrical structures of the world are so intimately connected (the metric after all determines the straight line) that the metrical field will of necessity become flexible as soon as the inertial field is deprived of its geometric rigidity.[18]

He has completed the movement away from myth and ritual. He has endorsed the notion of the world as an energy system, championed methodology, and taken the principles of geometry as the principles of poetry. Olson has extended Melville's world into a new arena of poetics.

III

Melville's dedication to scholarship, of informing his own vision with available materials on the subject, finally was the major influence on Olson. It became a matter of methodology, and then of form. THE MAXIMUS POEMS are grounded in historical, mythological and geological facts; they bring into themselves various information from the past and present. Olson, with the authority of Shakespeare and Melville behind him, discovered the means of making the past usable. First discovering that Hesiod and John White were contemporaries of the poem because they re-enacted primal events, and then taking them as congruent forms realizing a common energy, Olson was able to insert their views (and lots of other views too) into the historical situation, and thus compose a structure which defies logical narrative, but which, like MOBY-DICK, entertains multiple elements and procedures of structure within an intricate system of internal tensions. The following passage from "Projective Verse" could derive from the field action and configuration of MOBY-DICK:

...every element in an open poem (the syllable, the line, as well as the image, the sound, the sense) must be taken up as participants in the kinetic of the poem just as solidly as we are accustomed to take what we call the objects of reality; and that these elements are to be seen as creating tensions of a poem just as totally as do those other objects create what we know as the world.   (HU 56)

The fictive voice of Maximus, like Ishmael, becomes a means of "getting rid of the lyrical interference of the individual as ego" (HU 59), but of making him a medium for the spatial adjustment of elements so that the poet (via his figure) participates in the world he creates. The whole is realized in terms of Whitehead's corollary: "That no event/is not penetrated, in intersection or collision with, an eternal/event (M-IV 79).

Far more than simply borrowing the techniques of giving lists of provisions (MD 443, M 118-19), or just mentioning Melville (M 18), or referring to his novels (AM 114, M-3 94, 204), Olson's attitudes as a poet were forged from his engagement with Melville.[19] He wrote to Cid Corman:

> and why Melville & Homer &
> Shakespeare have been my masters (however much so many
> think Pound is)[20]

Olson at various times brings parts of Melville into the poem; for example, in "Letter 3" he writes:

> whose slaver
> would keep you off the sea, would keep you local,
> my Nova Scotians,
> Newfoundlanders,
> Sicilianos,
> Isolatos

> 4

> Isolated person, in Gloucester, Massachusetts, I, Maximus, address you
> you islands
> of men and girls
>
> (M 12)

when Melville had written:

> How it is, there is no telling, But Islanders seem to make the best whale-
> men. They were nearly all Islanders in the Pequod, *Isolatoes* too, I call
> such, not acknowledging the common continent of men, but each *Isolato*
> living on a separate continent of his own.[21]   (MD 118)

Melville's statement strengthens the stance of Maximus as the voice of the poem in these lines, while the reference to "the Divine Inert" (MD 144).

> inert of
> nature (the Divine
> Inert, the literary man
> of these men
> of the West
>
> (M 122)

helps define the condition of settlement being set out in the poem. The verification of the poem's position occurs also in "The Song and Dance of," when Olson reworks lines from Melville's JOURNAL UP THE STRAITS he had cited earlier:

> Venus
>
> does not arise from
>
> these waters. Fish
>
> do.
>
> (M 57-58)

THE EPILOGUE of the '56 JOURNAL. Off Cyprus, on his way from The Holyland to Greece, Melville can no more imagine a Venus to have risen from those waters than "on Mt Olivet that from there Christ rose."
(CMI 105)

Just as Christ had removed the mythological necessity of black magic from Melville's world, the economic factor of fishing and fur trading removes the presence of myth from Gloucester. This is one sort of verification, and another comes up in the poem "The Distances," when Olson cites the "hotel de Cluny" and "thorned on Torsoes" (MD 183), to support the notion that one must look into the deepest portions of a speculation or a historical building, for he may discover that, like the Hotel de Cluny, which was built on Roman baths, which were themselves built on older structures, it might be possible to find the very images (in this case statues) to bridge the distance between past and present. And of course, the final lines of MAXIMUS IV, V, VI

> I set out now
> in a box upon the sea
> (M-IV 203)

refer directly to Ishmael floating away from the sinking of the Pequod on Queequeg's coffin, indicating that Maximus has survived the attempts to recreate himself in the course of the volume, and now is ready to launch out on the final third of the voyage a ripened observer.

If Whitehead was the abiding spirit of Olson's poetry, then Melville was the informing spirit. Olson studied and admired Melville longer than any single writer; and at each point in his career, his development as a poet, he returned to Melville, as his base, to test and rediscover the validity of the new position in terms of the novels, mainly MOBY-DICK. It was not to imitate, but to learn that Olson went to Melville. In the journey back to

Melville, Olson made the longer journey back to primal reality and then moved forward to the present bringing the certainty that all history was alive in the act of the imagination. Uncovering it required a methodology. And Melville provided an example which made it possible for Maximus to spread out his map with language and measures purified and distinctive.

[1] Alfred North Whitehead, MODES OF THOUGHT (1938; New York, The Free Press, 1966), pp 6-7.

[2] All citations to Olson's work will be to the following books. Notes will be included in the text with the noted abbreviations. ARCHAEOLOGIST OF MORNING (London: Cape Goliard Press, in association with Grossman Publishers, 1970) as AM; CALL ME ISHMAEL: A STUDY OF MELVILLE (1947; London: Jonathan Cape, 1967) as CMI; HUMAN UNIVERSE AND OTHER ESSAYS, ed. Donald Allen (1965; New York: Grove Press, 1967) as HU; THE MAXIMUS POEMS (New York: Jargon/Corinth Books, 1960) as M; MAXIMUS POEMS IV, V, VI (London: Cape Goliard, in association with Grossman Publishers, 1968) as M-IV; THE MAXIMUS POEMS, VOLUME THREE, ed. Charles Boer and George Butterick (New York: Grossman Publishers, 1975) as M-3; "Lear and Moby-Dick," Twice A Year, I (Fall-Winter 1938) as L&MD; IN ADULLAM'S LAIR (Provincetown, Mass: To the Lighthouse Press, 1975) as IAL. Ann Charters, OLSON/MELVILLE: A STUDY IN AFFINITY (Berkeley: Oyez, 1968), as O/M. Olson's unpublished essays, "Exodus," will be indicated by E, and "Genesis" by G. All passages from Charles Olson's unpublished papers are copyrighted by the University of Connecticut and are quoted here with the permission of the University of Connecticut. Such passages will be indicated by the abbreviation UC in the text. All references to MOBY-DICK will be to MOBY-DICK, OR, THE WHALE, ed. Luther S. Mansfield and Howard P. Vincent (New York: Hendricks House, 1962), and also included in the text as M.D.

[3] Charles Olson, THE SPECIAL VIEW OF HISTORY, ed. Ann Charters (Berkeley, Oyez, 1970), pp. 23-24.

[4] Marjorie Perloff, "Charles Olson and the 'Inferior Predecessors': 'Projective Verse' Revisited," ELH, XL, 2 (Summer 1973), 285-306, esp. 306.

[5] In another sense, Olson's struggle with Pound's ego, his sense of time and the structure of the CANTOS, as well as his struggle with Williams' positive example of the local in PATERSON, yet his negative example of refusing to trace the roots of the city back to ancient sources indicates not so much Olson's single-minded indebtedness to Pound and Williams as his efforts to introduce their worlds into the form already defined by Poe and Melville.

"Williams is like Melville," Olson wrote, "a man who registers the going-ons of all of the human beings he lives among. He sees charge in them, worth in their fires, also a fire his own burns in, as against Ezra Pound, with that selection out of, that 'light in the conversations of—the letters of—the intelligent ones,' or at least the literate ones" (HU 112). Olson's central statements about his examination of Pound and Williams' poetics are in the letters to Robert Creeley, collected as MAYAN LETTERS. For another discussion of the subject which takes no account of Olson's long involvement with Melville see Robert von Hallberg, "Olson's Relation to Pound and Williams," CONTEMPORARY LITERATURE, XV, 1 (Winter 1974), 15-48.

[6] Martin Pops, "Melville: To him, Olson," BOUNDARY 2, II, 1/2 (Fall 73/Winter 74), 59, 61.

[7] The three essays, which exist in various original typed copies and carbon copies, were stored together, and all were water damaged to such an extent that the missing sections of "Exodus" and "Genesis" are now welded together into a hard little bundle.

[8] Perhaps it is impossible to determine the precise origin of Maximus as the center of consciousness and the maker of the poems. The Odysseus figure from the early CANTOS of Ezra Pound or the figure of Paterson in W.C. Williams' poem are as important as sources as the evolving self in Whitman's SONG OF MYSELF. There is the connection with Maximus of Tyre as a fact, but I seriously doubt the close affiliation claimed by Frank Davey, who also claims in the same article: "The evidence suggests strongly that Maximus of Gloucester is not a person but a metaphor" ("Six Readings of Olson's MAXIMUS," BOUNDARY 2, II, 1/2 (Fall 73/Winter 74), 291-321, esp. 291). The evidence indicates that Maximus is everything but a rhetorical figure. The assumption behind the evocation "Call me Ishmael" is something like—for the duration of the telling of this tale of Ahab and Moby-Dick please call me (Melville) Ishmael even though you (the audience) know that I (Melville) am telling/writing it. The same assumption operates in assuming for the duration of the poems that Maximus is not Olson, but a separate voice of the poems, dealing out the information and the perceptions. And Olson himself specified the stance of his voice: "It is not I,/even if the life appeared/biographical" ("Maximus of Gloucester," M-3, 101). Both Olson and Melville were able to create centers of perception inside their works to introduce information into the poem (in that sense Maximus is just as much a "Sub-Sub-Librarian" as Ishmael (without the necessity of justifying that inclusion, and finally to develop a methodology of endorsing particulars as participants in eternal processes. The form of MOBY-DICK and THE MAXIMUS POEMS is generated by the perceiving narrator, from within, and in its great diversity of elements, controls intricately woven connections.

Both narrators, in addition, create a grand stage for the action, and both are participants in the action they describe.

[9] George Butterick suggests that Dahlberg rejected these essays because they were "too 'Biblical' (meaning a style too much like his own" (IAL [iv]). With this passage as an example, it might be possible to suggest that the writing here is, frankly, Biblical, meaning that it imitates Biblical style.

[10] THE HISTORICAL LIBRARY OF DIODORUS THE SICILIAN, trans G. Booth, 2 vols. (London 1814) was one of Melville's principal sources for his information about Egyptian mythology, the other was Plutarch's essay "Isis and Osiris." Diodorus, like Freud who argues for the Egyptian origin of Moses, argues for Egypt as the origin place for the ancient gods and ideas about the gods. A pattern of imagery relates Ahab, the captain with the "Egyptian chest" (MD 182), to the Isis/Osiris myth. Olson would have known Melville's sources. I can speculate, or better, guess, that from his research on Melville Olson became acquainted with Egyptian myths, which show up, for example in "Maximus from Dogtown-1" and "In Cold Hell, in Thicket." Plutarch's *Moralia*, which contains the essay on Osiris, also contains the essay "The E at Delphi," which is a source for "The Kingfishers."

[11] See Donald Byrd, "For Complete Concentration," CREDENCES, I, 3 (May 1976), 101-114, esp 112-114.

[12] The idea of the lordship over nature, and then the exploitation of nature which resulted, lead naturally to the consideration of whaling as an economic factor. Olson implores: "Consider whaling as Frontier, and Industry" (CMI 23). The economic facts and information that went into the section "What Lies Under" come directly out of Olson's basic research. The direct sources are uncertain, but he did read and take over information from Karl Bramidt, WHALE OIL: AN ECONOMIC ANALYSIS. Olson's reading on the subject was extensive.

[13] While working on his thesis, Olson had found out that Melville's copy of Chase's NARRATIVE had been sold by the Anderson Galleries (later Parke-Bernet) on 9 February 1932. Howard Vincent, with additional information from David Randall, then of Scribners, and later of Indiana's Lilly Library, found the volume in the possession of Perc Brown. He passed the information on to Olson. In 1945 only one article had suggested that there might be two versions of MOBY-DICK, Leon Howard's "Melville's Struggle with the Angel, MLQ, I (June 1940), 195-206. The concept is fundamental to and fully developed in Vincent's study of Melville; Olson mentions it (CMI 25-38) and then makes no more use of. (Information confirmed in conversation with Howard Vincent 8 April 1976.)

¹⁴ The following is a partial listing of the direct and modified passages that come over from the essays into CALL ME ISHMAEL. This is not an exhaustive listing because my notes are unfortunately incomplete, and two of the essays are not available for study. "American Shiloh," CMI 41-L&MD 166; CMI 42-43-L&MD 167-169. "Lear and Moby-Dick," CMI 47-52-L&MD 167-171; CMI 51-L&MD 168, 172. "A Moby-Dick Manuscript," CMI 52-58-L&MD 172-178. "Ahab and His Fool," CMI 59-63-L&MD 178-182. "Shakespeare Concluded," CMI 64-69-L&MD 182-185; CMI 70-71-L&MD 187-188; CMI 72-L&MD 185; CMI 73-L&MD 189. "The book of the law of the blood," CMI 82-G 21; CMI 82-G 2, 21; CMI 83-G 7-8; CMI 85-G 12. "Christ," CMI 103-IAL 4; CMI 103-IAL 10; CMI 104-105-IAL 12-14. "Pacific Man," CMI 118-E 1. In light of these connections it is a little difficult to count as accurate Olson's comment that *Call Me Ishmael* had "no connection to the ms. of 1940 at all" (O/ M 9).

¹⁵ Charles Olson, LETTERS FOR ORIGIN: 1950-1955, ed. Albert Glover (London: Cape Goliard, in associate with Grossman Publishers, 1969), p. 70.

¹⁶ Vanderbeek writes: "I printed and did the printing in a little press at Blk Mt College—(also did silkscreen [   ] I think?). Larry Ht was a student? at Blk Mt who helped." (Letter to the author 30 October 1974). In a conversation August 1975 Ed Dorn said that he also remembered kicking copies of the poem out of the way so that he could close the door of the print shop. Martin Duberman, BLACK MOUNTAIN (AN EXPLORATION IN COMMUNITY) (New York: E.P. Dutton & Co., Inc., 1972), p. 336, says that Dorn printed the poem. Larry Hat(t) was at the college only in the summer of 1951. All attempts to find him have so far failed. The facts about the delivering of the "Letter" to the conference come from a letter to the author 28 September 1971 (UC).

¹⁷ The best essay on this subject is the one by Don Byrd, "The Possibility of Measure in Olson's MAXIMUS, BOUNDARY 2, II, 1/2 (Fall 73/Winter 74), 39-54.

¹⁸ Hermann Weyl, PHILOSOPHY OF MATHEMATICS AND NATURAL SCIENCE, trans. Olf Helmer (Princeton: Princeton University Press, 1949), pp. 105-06. Bernhard Riemann's article was printed in the journal GOTTINGEN ABHANDLUNGEN in 1854. It was later translated by W.K. Clifford as "On the Hypotheses Which Lie at the Bases of Geometry," NATURE, VIII (May 1, 1873), 14-17, 36-37. See Olson's re-vision (HU 122).

¹⁹ George Butterick notices a reference to MOBY-DICK, page 332, in the poem "His house/in the branches" (OLSON: THE JOURNAL OF THE CHARLES OLSON ARCHIVES, No. 4 (FAll 1975), 30). He also suggests in

the same number of OLSON that Olson refers to the chapter "The Tail" in "Maximus, to Gloucester, Letter 19 (A Pastoral Letter)."

[20] Letter cited from ORIGIN, third series, 20 (January 1971), 45.

[21] Earlier, (L&MD 187) Olson had written: "That vessel has a crew which is the census of the world. In the swift and skillful shift from 'Islanders' to 'Isolatoes' they change from a realistic crew to one highly symbolic." In the same essay Olson cites the passage from Melville's essay "Hawthorne and His Mosses" "... (as bronze was discovered by the melting of the iron and brass at the burning of Corinth)..." (L&MD 165), which comes into CALL ME ISHMAEL (pp. 38, 40) and into the poem "Some Good News":

> what is a proper fire
> is, it's what
> like Corinth
> burning down
> produces bronze—
> (M 123)

Siri Tuttle

The Stopping of the Battle
Syntactic Deviation in 3 Poems by Charles Olson

In the language of transformational syntax, a sentence is defined as ambiguous if it can be derived equally well from two or more deep structures. Whether or not a sentence is ambiguous is often a clue to ordering relationships in its derivation. If we accept Noam Chomsky's view (in *Aspects of the Theory of Syntax*) that transformations cannot introduce meaning-bearing elements, then an ambiguous sentence is only questionably grammatical because alternate meanings are possible.

Ambiguous sentences, however, are frequently "understood". This is also the case with other types of "ungrammaticality"; even though we may find a sentence unacceptable, we often understand it perfectly well. Sometimes an interpretation of such a sentence can be made by substituting a correct form for an incorrect one:

*The cat eaten the mouse.

This sentence can be understood by either substituting "ate" for "eaten", or inserting "has".

Other sentences can be understood metaphorically. Most metaphors are formed by violating a single selectional restriction: the sentence

I had to eat my words

would be ungrammatical if it were not a metaphor. It violates the selectional rule which regulates the concreteness of things which can be eaten. Even in unfamiliar cases of this kind of violation, however, we are usually able to assign an interpretation, as Chomsky has noted:

> Sentences that break selectional rules can often be interpreted metaphorically... or allusively in one way or another, if an appropriate context of greater or less complexity is supplied. That is, these sentences are apparently interpreted by a direct analogy to well-formed sentences that observe the selectional rules in question. Clearly, one would proceed in quite a different way if forced to assign an interpretation to sentences that break strict subcategorization rules..."

Strict subcategorization rules regulate the environment of verbs categorized as Transitive, Intransitive, pre-Adjective, etc. Sentence that break them, such as

I seemed the vase into little pieces

or

> I congeal that David will desire

seem to be interpretable "in quite a different way" but are more ambiguous than sentences which break selectional rules.

The interpretation of such sentences is central to the reading and writing of poetry. Selectional violations, as metaphors, appear in most "traditional" poetry, as well as in more modern works. More recently, poets have explored structures which violate strict subcategorization rules: (this line is from Dylan Thomas)

> I hug to love with my unruly scrawl. . .

The next order of magnitude in violations of grammar would seem to be major category violations: substitutions of nouns for verbs, adjectives for prepositions, etc. Although there are examples of this in Thomas also, e.e. cummings is the poet most famous for this type of structure:

> My father moved through dooms of love
> through sames of am through haves of give

"Am" and "give" are usually verbs, but here are placed as objects of the preposition "of".

As it approaches this more basic type of ungrammaticality, poetry becomes harder to interpret uniquely. Ambiguity proliferates with the increased violation of the semantic/syntactic rules described above. When syntax proper is disrupted, ambiguity is inevitable.

In the following analysis of three of Charles Olson's poems, I have concentrated on isolating strictly syntactic violations: jumbling of sentence elements, fragmentary sentences, etc. I have begun by selecting a possible meaning for each sentence (or two meanings, where the sentence is ambiguous): a "deep structure" for the poem. This allows analysis of the processes "between" pure meaning and the formalized poem. Some of these processes are English transformations; some are directly related to the form of the poem; i.e., a word's position in a line; some have to do with punctuation, which, though more orthographic than syntactic, can change interpretations in important ways. I am assuming that whatever ungrammaticality is found functions to further communication, not as purposeful obscurity.

In "Moonset," multiple ambiguities are created through the avoidance of conventional punctuation, specific placement of line-ends, and unorthodox capitalization. The first sentence

> Goodbye red moon

is unambiguous. The second has two possible interpretations:

1) In that color you set/ west of the Cut I should
   imagine/ forever Mother

Here "I should imagine" modifies "you set".

2) In that color you set west of the Cut
   I should imagine Mother forever

Here it is two sentences, one addressed to the moon, one a declaration of
what "I should imagine". The placement of "forever" heightens the ambiguity, as it fails to weight interpretation one way or the other. The identity of
the moon as mother is generated by ambiguity without direct metaphor.

The next sentence has three possibilities:

1) After 47 years this month/ a Monday at 0 am/
   you set

2) After 47 years this month/ a Monday at 9 am/
   you set, I rise

3) After 47 years this month/ a Monday at 9 am/
   you set, I rise, I hope

Each different reading will affect the reading of the next sentence, but
again, because there is no punctuation or implied punctuation to point to
one or another, each meaning is equally weighted.

If we take 1) for sentence 2, sentence 3 reads:

1) I rise I hope/ a free thing as probably/
   what you more were

or

1a) I rise I hope/ a free thing as probably/
    what you more were Not

If we take 2) for sentence 2, sentence 3 reads:

2) I hope/ a free thing as probably/
   what you more were

or

2a) ... what you more were Not

If we take 3) for sentence 2, sentence 3 reads:

3) a free thing as probably/ what you more were

or

3a) a free thing as probably/ what you more were Not

With 1), the implication is: "I am a free thing." With 2), it is "I hope (for) a free thing". With 3), it is "you were probably (Not) a free thing". These interpretations can exist simultaneously, with the exception of the acceptance or rejection of "Not".

"Not" can also have its domain in the next sentence:

1) Not/ the suffering one you sold/ sowed me on Rise

2) Not/ the suffering one you sold/ sowed me on

If "Not" is accepted as part of this sentence, it negates "sowed"; if it is rejected, it goes back to the sentence above it, and negates "were". This ambiguity of domain produces considerable tension between different structures. "Rise" can also switch domains, from "sowed me on Rise", where it is a noun, to "Rise/Mother from off me".

Line-end emphasis is important here too. If the poem read

. . . a free thing as probably
what you more were
Not the suffering one you sold
sowed me on
Rise Mother from off me

much ambiguity would be lost. In the absence of punctuation, line-ends appear to function as sentence ends, especially where the next line *looks* as if it begins a sentence. By placing "Not" and "Rise", capitalized, at line-end, Olson gives us an unweighted ambiguity which amounts to a paradox.

God damn you God damn me my
misunderstanding of you

is again ambiguous.

1) God damn you, God damn me. My understanding of you. . .

2) God damn you. God damn (to) me my misunderstanding of you.

The final line, separated by stanza break, is then almost unambiguous.

1) I can die now. I just begun to live.

2) I can die now (that) I just begun to live.

In summary, this poem is written in repeated patterns of ambiguity. Each sentence and line depends on the interpretation of the line previous for its interpretation. As a result there are multiple readings for the poem, each equally possible but subtly contradictory.

Three devices are responsible for this: avoidance of punctuation, which removes the possibility for deciding where a sentence ends; placement of emphasized words at line-ends; and capitalization of certain words such as "Not" and "Rise". Line-end placement and capitalization work together to allow these words to stand at either sentence end (as indicated by position in line), or sentence beginning (as indicated by capitalization).

One possible interpretation for the poem, given its structure, is that the conflicts in the sentences reflect the conflict between poet, moon and Mother, and most particularly the conflict between poet and self. If we accept this we are assuming that a "unity" exists between the content and the form of the poem. The poet may be choosing (intuitively or otherwise) a pattern of language which parallels grammatical ambiguity with the ambiguity of his emotional situation.

In "Letter 27," several devices occur: contrast in sentence length and structure; use of line-end as punctuation and emphasis; and unended sentences.

The first discrete segment of the poem is made up of three stanzas, each of which contains one sentence. The first and third sentences are long and complex, eight and nine lines, respectively. They are connected by commas and the breath spaces of line-ends. These stanzas have the detailed quality of oral story-telling.

> I was so young my first memory
> is of a tent spread to feed lobsters
> to Rexall conventioneers, and my father,
> a man for kicks, . . .

But this comfortable oral style is broken off abruptly:

> under one of those frame hats women then

> This, is no bare incoming
> of novel abstract form, this

This change is effected by several means: a shift from long stanzas to short; a shift in semantic content, from detailed narrative to abstract statement; and the omitted verb in the last line of the narrative.

Interestingly enough, on a tape of Olson reading made soon after the poem was finished, the verb is not omitted from the line, which reads:

> under one of those frame hats women then *wore*

the omission was then incorporated, as a revision, to emphasize the break-off of the narrative. The impression is that the narrative is infinite, and goes on under the abstract discussion like a radio turned down low so as not to interfere with conversation.

Olson's reading of this poem is especially interesting in the light of this transition and also of the final lines of the poem:

...I compell Gloucester
to yield, to
change
    Polis
is this

Generally, Olson ends stanzas in his reading with either a rising or a straight inflect (this type of reading is very common among poets reading their own work, but differs from the usual inflection of non-question sentences). "Wore", at the end of the third stanza, has a straight inflection; the transition is effected in the reading by a general slowing down of the voice and a gathering of intensity. Because the stanzas are shorter in the second section, rising inflections appear more often, and the tone pattern begins to resemble that of repeated questions.

In the last lines, quoted above, Olson allows himself a falling inflection on "Change"—a breath—"Polis", neither rising nor falling—a breath—"is this", a straight inflection (like "Polis"). He manages to retain the ambiguity of the line, which, because of its fragmentary nature and the placement of the verb before "this", could be either a question or a statement.

To hear the tape, however, is not to gather any new information about the poem. Olson reads so as to duplicate in his listeners, as much as possible, the experience of his reader. He does not resolve ambiguity. He uses his voice to emphasize transitions which have visual support from the design of the poem.

Two additional devices should be noted. One is used more importantly in Enyalion: the placement of key words at line end instead of line beginning.

This, is no bare incoming
of novel abstract form, *this*

is no welter or the forms
of those events, *this*,

Greeks, is the stopping
of the battle

The first "this", coming as transition out of the narrative into the discussion, is emphasized by the unorthodox use of the comma. It needs this emphasis in order to be understood properly as referring to the transition itself. The second "this" is emphasized by a comma preceding it and by its placement at line-end: two devices. The third "this" is set off by two commas, preceding and following, and by placement at line-end. The repetition and increased emphasis of "this", as well as the number of them (three: the magic rhetorical number) give the word the status—not of pronoun—but of pro-transition, pro-stanza.

The other device also has to do with this transition. Semantically, the first of the three sentences is ambiguous, hinging on the word "bare". This could mean "naked", modifying "incoming", or it could mean something closer to "barely", a type of negative. In the latter case, the domain of "bare" is the entire sentence. Since there is already a negative present—"no"—the effect of this ambiguity is to confuse the message:

This is not (but just barely not) an incoming

The next sentence continues the confusion, by allowing the reader to choose between three possibilities for the equivalence of "this": "this is no welter", "this is not the forms of those events", or "this is the forms of those events". The repetition of "form", a semantically loose word with many possible meanings, muddies the picture further.

The final sentence, however, snaps back to precision and certainty. "This, Greeks, is the stopping of the battle". *That* is what it is. The effect of this certainty is heightened by the preceding muddle; the stopping of the battle is clarified by contrast with the uncertain image above.

That "this" turns out to be "the stopping of the battle" suggests additional support for "this" being also the transition from the first section of the poem to the next. There is a level of self-consciousness to this: the poet talking about the poetry as he writes it. "I am stopping the battle. I am turning off the radio that plays old reminiscences. I am turning off the arguing mind. Watch: I am going to start talking a different way. There will be NO MORE WAR between what I say and what really is true."

The "meaning" of those transitional lines is hard to figure from the words that make them up. If we allow "metalinguistic" statements to be part of the meaning of the poem, then the transition and what it implies are of great importance to an understanding of the poet's view of language. The transition made is from conversational language to an attempt at a real "novel abstract form". This form is being created as we read; as it muddles its way into focus, we find it and a message about it simultaneously. We participate in the creation of this form by our sympathetic struggle to understand what it says.

"Enyalion," the third of the poems, utilizes all the devices described above: ambiguity by displacement, use of line-end as emphasis and punctuation, unended sentences. In addition, it uses a specific inversion of subject and verb to create unweighted ambiguity and emphasis of the noun.

The first sentence—and stanza—is made ambiguous by this type of displacement. If "rages" is taken as a verb, then it and "strain" are inverted from their normal syntactic position, and thus emphasized. Each is also alone in its line, a strong emphatic device. The sentence can be understood with this interpretation, but the reading is fragmentary and abrupt:

Dog of Tartarus rages
Guards of Tartarus strain
Finks of the Bosses, War Makers strain

If "rages" is a noun, then the sentence is easier to read literally:

Rages strain Dog. . . Guards. . . Finks. . . War Makers. . .

The meaning is not much changed. Nevertheless, a tension is set up by the need to make a decision about the function of "rages". Taken either way, "rages" and "strain" are words which will contrast violently with the words associated with Enyalion.

With the word "not" in the first line of the second stanza, the structure shifts abruptly. "Not Enyalion". The negative has as domain the entire first stanza, particularly the verb or verbs. Enyalion is first defined negatively as the opposite of the nouns in the first stanza. His name is emphasized at its first appearance by one of the simplest possible devices—repetition. It also, here and almost everywhere else in the poem, appears at the ends of lines. Because of the repetition of this structure, there is a constant relaxed ambiguity.

Enyalion
has lost his hand, Enyalion
is beautiful, Enyalion

If we follow the lines sequentially, the "Enyalion" at the line end always has as verb the beginning of the line following. If we separate lines, there is a repeated inversion of subject and verb which, in this case, because it places the subject at line-end, functions to emphasize the noun further. There is no tension to this; tension is released at "Not Enyalion" and does not build up again until the last stanza.

Verbs of being are omitted.

far far out into Eternity Enyalion
the law of possibility, Enyalion

the beautiful one, Enyalion

The effect is to further de-emphasize the verb in relation to Enyalion; to make him even more a picture, *image* as opposed to *action*.

44

Repetition of these words and structures is also important:

Enyalion
war
brown-red
picture
possibility
beauty
earth
shine (noun)

All are nouns, or, like "brown-red", noun-adjectives. The repeating structure is this:

Noun Phrase
Verb Phrase—Noun Phrase

This structure, with changes of lexical choice, is repeated with little variation until the last stanza, which is a lengthy sentence fragment having no subject or verb. There is a change in the landscape: after seeing Enyalion close up, we recede to a larger picture. The shift in structures assists, as does the use of words different from the repeated nouns of the major part of the poem.

This final stanza is also important because it is a fragment, a non-ending. It is similar in intention to the unended sentences in *Letter 27* and the uninflection or rising inflection of Olson's reading of line and stanza ends on the tape. Interestingly, his reading of this poem ends with a falling inflection on the last words, "over man". In this case, however, the sentence is too unsettled and fragmentary to be completed by an inflection. Olson thus takes no risk of losing his non-ending when he reads the lines with this inflection—it is, in fact, ungrammatical in context.

If poetry is language—and if language is intended to communicate (both positions are arguable, as evidenced by recent theoretical work)—then poetry is intended to communicate. In neither ordinary language nor poetry can we communicate by pure meaning—if we are to be understood, meaning must pass through structure. The metaphor of deep and surface structure used by linguists is applicable to poetry in this sense. Surface structure in language might be defined as that point in the generation of the utterance when meaning is most communicable. If surface structure in poetry is defined also as its most communicable stage, then a range of structures appears to be acceptable—from somewhere "below" the level of prose surface structure to somewhere "above" it. The levels "above" are those reached by application of special poetic "transformations".

I have assumed that poetry is a "special" type of language, derived mostly from the elements and rules operative in ordinary language. Where a sentence in poetry deviates from the standard of well-formed sentences in English, I assume that it is "derivatively generated" in the terms of the definition given in *Aspects:*

> A natural terminological decision would be to say that the grammar directly generates the language consisting of just the sentences that do not deviate at all... with their structural descriptions. The grammar derivatively generates all other strings... with their structural descriptions. These structural descriptions will indicate the manner and degree of deviance of the derivatively generated sentences.

The "derivatively generated" sentences in the three poems here analyzed are the product of two processes: the non-application of some transformations operative in English; and the application of derived rules peculiar to the poet (or the poem, in some cases). These rules are extrapolated from English-language rules or conventions of traditional poetry.

If we rewrite the second stanza of "Enyalion" as a prose sentence (choosing one possible meaning) we might get:

Enyalion, who has lost his hand and is beautiful,
has shown himself to be the High King and a War
Chief.

The difference between the poetry and this paraphrase lies in the application of certain transformations: relative clause formation (which is selectively deleted in the poem) and equivalent noun phrase deletion (which is selectively ignored in the poem). Olson has, in the place of these two applicable transformations, applied two of his own—line-end placement and optional deletion of verbs of being. In one sense, then, the lines are an intermediary structure of the grammar—an unfinished sentence. In another sense, since they have their own private transformations, they are finished but exist as examples of a different dialect of English—one where equivalent noun phrases do not have to be deleted and verbs of being may be. They are also ambiguous. The paraphrase above is not the only possible one, for a different placement of the verb of being gives a different meaning. This ambiguity is mostly structural, however; the choice of meanings it offers is narrow and these meanings do not contradict each other. (Contrast this with the ambiguity in "Moonset", which has the possibility of multiple contradictions.)

The lines from "Enyalion" display a surface structure a little "below" prose surface structure. The apparent reason for that position is that another structure has been set up which renders prose surface structure impossible. This is the *noun phrase/ verb phrase-noun phrase* structure which has been noted to occur throughout the poem.

On such short acquaintance with a poet (three poems is very few to analyze) it is probably impossible to say much about the relationship of structure to meaning without being superficial and presumptuous. Within poems, hypotheses may be offered which may be valid for those poems. But to understand a work requires more than a careful combing of its syntactic structures; syntax is only one component of a grammar.

Where a poet has been credited with (or accused of) meta-linguistic statements, however (and Olson has), such a combing is the only way to verify or disprove that claim. Precisely how structural ambiguity can be paralleled with emotional ambiguity is a subject for a much longer study, one that can take psychological as well as linguistic factors into account.

Richard Grossinger

The Four Badlands

Original Course Outline:

Reading List

A— Prairie

James Fenimore Cooper: *The Prairie*
Carl Sauer : "Conditions of Pioneer Life in the Upper Illinois Valley"
    "The Barrens of Kentucky"
    "Homestead and Community on the Middle Border"

B— Arctic Regions and the Moon

James Fenimore Cooper: *The Sea Lions*
Elisha Kent Kane: *Arctic Explorations in Search of Sir John Franklin*
Charles Francis Hall: *Arctic Researches and Life Among the Esquimaux*
Richard K. Nelson: *Hunters of the Northern Ice*
Richard Grossinger: *The Continents* (connecting Arctic regions to the Moon)
Carlos Casteneda: *The Teachings of Don Juan*, etc. (connecting the Moon to the prairie)
Michael Collins: *Carrying the Fire*

C— Ocean

Herman Melville: *Moby Dick*
Charles Olson: *The Maximus Poems*
Christopher Columbus: *Journals*
Geoffrey Ashe: *Lands to the West*

D— City

Le Roi Jones: *The System of Dante's Hell*
            Tales
Mario Puzo: *Fortunate Pilgrim*
Edward Dorn: *Gunslinger* (as language, not as landscape)
Jack Kerouac: *On the Road*

The Archetypal Sea

Homer himself strains against the mists of the Mediterranean to reach the Atlantic, to send Odysseus to the margins of the known universe.

And Cyrus Gordon[1] (arguing out of the Amarna renaissance of the Near East) reminds us that long before Homer, Semites were in Brazil, Phoenicians kin to Trojans trading with South American Indians. Pre-Biblical writing in New World jungles remains. The voyages continued through the time of Homer: Roman coins have been found in Tennessee.

By Sauer's premise (in *Northern Mists*), picked up in Olson's *Maximus*, the European mind continues to project an archetypal Mediterranean onto the Atlantic long after an Atlantic is known. The wild northern ocean comes to contain the lost and spiritual sites of the Western mind: Atlantis, Circê's Island, the Tribes of Israel, the Gate to the Underworld, the Passage to lands in the sky. It is the sea of the Irish "Brendan" voyages and the Norse sagas, of Columbus' journals and Shakespeare's *Tempest*. The actual condition of geographical knowledge changes, but the gnostic and Indo-European endures, right out into the Sioux villages and Australian outback. The cryptic remains of those who settled on these shores in ancient times become (for us) clues in the quest itself that they were on. Their bones and hearths, in the reversal of time, are the very artifacts that would have told them where they were.

Cyclops is the forge-keeper at Hekla,[2] whose residue is the puzzle at Belle Isle, Newfoundland, becomes Sasquatch of the Northern woods. The signs of this "fiction," which is as old a non-fiction as the Golden Age, the lost continent, and Palaeolithic man, precede the Indo-European onto the prairie, where Holocene flora and fauna is as abundant as in any France or Spain, and where the Tibeto-Indians, the descendants of Magdelanian cavemen, are only the latest previous human migrants. But they recall, within the canons of anthropological reconstruction, our brothers in the pre-Homeric text. They are the inhabitants of Cooper's tales, not his Delaware and New York Indians, but the furthest extent of his *Prairie* and *Oak Openings*,[3] where the Biblical landscape begins to crumble under the authenticity of a glacial event.

When Cleveland and Detroit rule a demystified prairie, the Poles are recovered from old Greek cosmographies, which placed Arctic regions with the Moon as additional continents, reachable only with charms and lore. (Olson's Pytheas, the lost Viking sagas, and Kepler's *Somnium*). The science fiction of our imagined planetary and galactic voyages remains a remote casting for an Indo-European homeland, where the myths and fantasy-creatures match, and the tales merge with the mountains beside which they were first recovered from another darkness. All the planets of all the great suns and stars are Celtic, Gothic, Pictish, Hittite. If we need a justification, we write one into the tale, we say the real hearthland is in outer space somewhere, that our fathers left us to people this planet, an event of which we have no objective memory because it does not fall in the possible range of objective time. If this cover is a hoax, then DNA could always be from another world, bearing in its chemical "memory" the seed-strands of events of another creation.

Our space voyages are Frederick Cook and Admiral Peary on Ice Age planets,[4] Lewis and Clark exploring worlds as big as America once was, Columbus again, Brendan and Homer again, setting out into seas so unknown, so purely attached to creation at the treadle, that anything could appear in them, anything that we have ever imagined, even by failing to imagine, in the vastness of our migration. We are involved once again in the movement of peoples from the old mountains to the sea of a fantastic civilization of boat-people and pyramids, who have wondrous machines of writing and communication; we reconceive the flight of Celtic peoples from their homeland in Gaul to the remote shores of Britanny, burying their coins by the tens of thousands as they go. Our imagination of Atlantis and a Pacific archipelago is almost racial by now, and we must understand that it is only in *fact*, in no other way, that it does not change. The new man of IBM may consider the badlands a mythology only, but they are less a mythology than his cities and computers and space voyages, for they are the sole condition that guides him and sends him where he may go.

Difference Between a Man-Produced and a
Naturally-Occurring Badland

Prairie, Ocean, Arctic, Moon, and City form a circle of paradoxical extremes. If we consider the prairie a naturally barren zone, settled by the same technology that allowed cities to be laid on top of farmlands, we must also consider that the prairies, as found by the Europeans, were the results of Indian fires. It is the city which makes the prairie and ocean again uninhabitable.

Is the ocean a badland or a garden? If badlands, it is so only as limitation, as guardian of history and director of migration, as separator of cultures, source of unintelligibility and alien invaders. Ocean is also blender of vastly disperse ecological zones: Gulf Stream, glaciermelt, fish breeder, life source, ebb tide settler.

The Arctic is the place to which the Ice Ages recede, bearing all seeds and holding in suspended animation the genetics of all possible worlds and cultures, direct ancestor of middle Paleolithic (Acheulian) peoples. In the heart of ice is fire, without which it would still be African Genesis.

The Moon and other planets, as well as the interplanetary interstellar belt, play to the Earth as biosphere what the Ice Ages play to the Earth's climates. They are raw condition, the uncongealed temperate garden. They are what the Earth was and what the Earth will become.

Biological Limits

Man in his natural state cannot settle Jupiter (though, with Darwinian selection as the law, Jovian life emerges by the same lock and key arrangement from the Jovian elements). Habitat is amicable and temperate because organism and environment are indistinguishable, their lattices enmeshed in DNA or any other *I Ching* chemistry. The prairie, the Arctic regions, the ocean, the planets are all endless summers, paradises, to their natives. But everyone, since, has been marched to reservations, everyone except the smallest bugs, rotifers, volvoxes, and coyotes who return to New England. Even the city is potential Eden, to the mutant now being born (Chardin claims is the mind, and its niche: the noosphere; the regionalists call corporate global nonsense). It might also be new urban bacteria.

Reading list: one book—Carl Sagan: *Intelligent Life in the Universe*; see especially chapters entitled "The Physical Setting for the Origin of Life" and "Chemical Syntheses and Early Evolution of Life," his ultraviolet fangs awakening an elemental sea. It is as precise as a prayer-stick, as brilliantly reasoned, whether it is true or not.

Carl Sauer ("Theme of Plant and Animal Destruction in Economic History")[5] takes it from the other end: prairie becomes desert, Mesopotamia and Kansas-Iowa leached, barren. Technological chemistry is not alchemy, cannot alter elemental structure. Deterioration beyond a certain point is absolute; colonialism *can* overextend, even in the guise of multi-national countries and global resource-use. And R. Buckminster Fuller: 92 essential elements, in continuously changing, recurring patterns, no possible pollution.[6]

Footnote to the Ecological Minimum

From asceticism and deprivation comes a spiritual and mythological richness. In the barest environments man turns the big corners (not in California orchards). Where outer resources dwindle even to senselessness, inner resources return from a fire within (to which the twentieth century has denied a legal name, and so bastardized for its length): the Tibetan cave-saints, the painters and dancers of Lascaux, Cabeza de Vaca and not De Soto or Coronado, finally even Frederick Cook and Michael Collins.

The Prairie (Sauer and Cooper)

The Prairie as Ocean

The experience of the vast plain, like a sea of grass, pastured upon by great herds of buffalo, was vividly recalled. Jaramillo noted at first they saw bulls in number (aged and immature males apart from the herds), but soon found themselves "among a vast mass of cows, calves, and bulls, all intermingled... There are so many that I do not know with what to compare them except to the fish in the sea, because as well on this journey as on the one thereafter, made by the whole force on its way to Quivira, there were so many that often we passed through their midst and though we wished to take another way we could not do so, the plains being covered with them. Their meat is as good to eat as beef of Castille, and some think it better. The bulls are large and brave and do not attack readily."[a] A second anonymous account told that four days' journey beyond Cibola they "came to land as level as the sea, in which plains there are innumerable cattle like those of Castille, some larger. The land is so flat that men get lost if they draw apart by half a league. Thus one horseman was lost, as were two saddle horses. There remains no trace of where one has gone and for this reason they had recourse to marking the road with buffalo dung, there being no stones or anything else." Castaneda also said that markers of buffalo bones and dry dung were made by the advance scouts to guide the main party.[b] Carl Sauer: "The Journey of Coronado (1540-1542)[11] in *Sixteenth Century North America.*

From the summits of the swells, the eye became fatigued with the sameness and chilling dreariness of the landscape. The earth was not unlike the ocean when its restless waters are heaving heavily after the agitation and fury of the tempest have begun to lessen. There was the same waving and regular surface, the same absence of foreign objects, and the same boundless extent to the view. Indeed so very striking was the

---

[a] Compare Melville's description of a ship among nursing whales.

[b] There is an obvious similarity to lobster traps, i.e., the difficulty of marking and remembering a spot at sea.

resemblance between the water and the land that however much the geologist might sneer at so simple a theory, it would have been difficult for a poet not to have felt that the formation of the one had been pro-duced by the subsiding dominion of the other. Here and there a tall tree[c] rose out of the bottoms, stretching its naked branches aborad like some solitary vessel; and to strengthen the delusion, far in the distance appeared two or three rounded thickets looking in the misty horizon like islands resting on the waters. James Fenimore Cooper: *The Prairie.*

Note also in Cooper the continuous images of waves, the characters becoming lost in open spaces, and the parties easily boarded and raided (as ships at sea). Cooper reaches forward to Sauer and backward to Shakespeare and Homer. His prairie-ocean is obscure, though partly only to his own intelligence, which is still greater than most of his contemporaries. He has no magical islands or mythological peoples, but his geneaology is accurately Sioux and Pawnee, with their own traditional wisdom, a wisdom that comes through more in landscape than lore. The real event of the book is the prairie, not the people; it lays the conditions by which they live and are separated; it is the function by which vultures, buffalo, Indians, squatters, trappers, and settlers circle each other through interlocked zones. Sioux in chase of buffalo, spied upon by Ishmael and his brood, Pawnee tracking Sioux, the "buzzards looking down for their food; and it behoves us, as Christian men who have so much at stake, to look down upon them both." Cooper's "prairie life."

The prairie is a New World theogony in which fragments of an unknown creation burst into the Western mind, which receives them in a dated theology. The Louisiana Purchase (on which the book opens and before which the West was another nation's wilderness) is followed by the Lewis and Clark Expedition, which the book parallels.

> An hour sufficed to bring the fugitives to the bank of the stream, which was one of the hundred rivers that serve to conduct, through the mighty arteries of the Missouri and Mississippi, the waters of that vast and still uninhabited region to the ocean.

Uninhabited! Even Dr. Battius intuits otherwise, and he tries to make a European text, a Linnaean subsystem, with homage to Buffon, out of its richness of species. The Sioux read him as he comes to them and dress him up in the language he speaks.

> He had been despoiled of his upper garments, and in their stead his

---

[c] It was on such a tree that Abiram White was to hang, and his screams to echo through the prairie, like the ghost of one who walked the plank.

body was sufficiently protected from the cold by a fantastically painted robe of dressed deerskin. As if in mockery of his pursuit, sundry toads, frogs, lizards, butterflies, etc., all duly prepared to take their places at some future day in his own private cabinet, were attached to the solitary lock on his head, to his ears, and to various other conspicuous parts of his person.

A Prospero further reduced by the real dangers of a New World, the actuality of its relics and implements quite apart from Europe's own lost wizardry. No longer are the symbols even alive for such doctors and anthropologists, so they are hung as dead forms on their robes, like the pictures of suns and moons Robert Kelly speaks of in "The Alchemist."[7] The wizard is unaware that all which stands for living process is first and foremost alive. So the Indians transcend their classification and capture the scientist.

"Look about you, man;" says the trapper to Dr. Battius. "Where are the multitudes that once peopled these prairies, the kings and palaces, the riches and the mightinesses of this desert?"

Battius laughs. He knows there are no ancient North American kingdoms, no monuments. He asks the trapper to show him the "columns, catacombs, and pyramids standing amid the sands of the East like wrecks on a rocky shore. . ."

But Cooper is not trying to prove a theory of archaeology; he has no point of view about New World civilizations, one way or the other. He is responding to a sentience and immediacy in the air, the implicit and obscure certainty that something large has been here and is gone, be it a race of spirits, Indians, Hebrews, or Jovians.

Like Melville, Cooper asks: Where did they go? And in the best passage in the book, he gives us a code for the whirl of nature and time: tree rings = circles = paths = cycles of the Earth through the seasons = buffalo changing his coat = fresh horns coming from buck's skull = visible discontinuous code.

The trapper replies:

"They are gone. Time has lasted too long for them. For why? Time was made by the Lord, and they were made by man. This very spot of reeds and grass on which you now sit may once have been the garden of some mighty king. It is the fate of all things to ripen and then to decay. The tree blossoms and bears its fruit, which falls, rots, withers, and even the seed is lost! Go, count the rings of the oak and of the sycamore; they lie in circles, one about another, until the eye is blinded in striving to make out their numbers; and yet a fall change of the seasons comes round while the stem is winding one of these little lines about itself, like the buffalo changing his coat or the buck his horns; and what does it all amount to?"

The American Prairie as Real Estate

Cooper: Prairie defined as universal history in epic time and space.

> Virtually the whole of this immense region is a plain. For a distance extending nearly fifteen hundred miles east and west, and six hundred north and south, there is scarcely an elevation worthy to be called a mountain. Even hills are not common, though a good deal of the face of the country has more or less of that 'rolling' character, which is described in the opening pages of this work.
>
> There is much reason to believe that the territory which now composes Ohio, Illinois, Indiana, Michigan, and a large portion of the country west of the Mississippi lay formerly under water. The soil of all the former states has the appearance of an alluvial desposit, and isolated rocks have been found of a nature and in situations which render it difficult to refute the opinion they they have been transferred to their present beds by floating ice. This theory assumes that the Great Lakes were the deep pools of one immense body of freshwater which lay too low to be drained by the irruption that laid bare the land. "Introduction."

Sauer: Prairie as each microenvironmental plot of ground, separate histories and separate potentials.

Cooper: The prairie is habitable only by residual humanity in dire and symbolic conditions. Sauer: Underneath the temporary covering of tough grasses and sod are the ingredients of incredible fertility.

Cooper: Water visible only as a mirage. Sauer: Water accessible by wells just below the surface.

Cooper: Prairie as a hangout for those whose way of life is being destroyed: like a slum, or a Last Chance café. Sauer: Prairie as the undeveloped land for a new way of life.

Cooper: Wandering squatters, trappers, Boones, broken Indian tribes. Sauer: Frontiersmen, inventors, farmers, investors.

Cooper: Healthy land, almost Biblical longevity of individuals and peoples. Sauer: Initially a land of fevers, diseases, plagues, bad drainage, Hobbesian.

Cooper: Nostalgia for western wilderness; Natty Bumppo begins on the coast of New England and flees the hatchets and settlements by following the frontier. Sauer: Nostalgia for eastern civilization, European village life; the expectation is that village defines the outlying farms, not that the farms are isolated pockets from which a village grows. Homesickness is a disease.

Cooper: Indians and whites meet as powerful individuals in universal time. Sauer: The settlers come west too late (and bearing too much liquor) for there to be any real cultural sharing or learning.

Cooper: Fire on the prairie as a device of the plot, changing the fates of the characters and tribes involved. Sauer: Fire on the prairie an example of the major disruptive effect pre-technological man can have on an environment. Both agree that the landscape is tinder and man is the match.

1850: one year before the death of Cooper. 1850: Sauer's date for the introduction of agricultural machinery which will make the prairie habitable.

Arctic Regions and The Moon[8]

> "Why this constant succession of blizzards and all this needless hardship for men seeking food for themselves and those they care for. Why? Why?" Aua, the Eskimo shaman.[9]

The Arctic regions lie prior to America (as the Illinois and Wisconsin glaciations of the Pleistocene), and beyond America (literally, Alaska and the Northwest Territories) as the frontier at which habitation thins out. North America *was* ice during the early periods of Indian migration from Eurasia, and America becomes ice again when its conditions are stretched back to that severity (the oil pipeline, Cooper's island of seals, the Moon voyages, unheated ghettoes).

Because Arctic regions are brutal ecologically, they become temples of man's conversion (in *The Sea Lions*, Roswell Gardiner has his conversion when he views the full span of heavenly bodies from his ship in polar waters;[10] Amundsen also has a cosmological awakening on the ice). Aua and Ivaluardjuk are in life-long proximity to an ice-demon who will not leave them in peace. It is not even an irony that the astronauts are the source of a Whole Earth consciousness with which they were sent out, in a military operation, to do battle.

Men return from the Artic mutilated, ruined, missing limbs. Parts of their body never work right again. They have been, unsuspecting, on visionquests. They have given up what has kept them from seeing, and in their famished state, their perception is sharpened to beyond what they know. They learn where America is, where the Earth is. Materialism creates the paradox for which it is the famous antidote. The drive for extension of space and resources becomes loss of real resources, and even of life. In *The Sea Lions*, the men are forced to destroy the wealth that drew them into the region in order to survive the winter. Deacon Pratt dies, passing beyond all worldly goods; at the moment the gold coins are put in his hands, his hands cease to feel. At the height of "prosperity," we destroy the material base, bringing back the ice, and worse. But in the first occasion of its coming, it was the guardian of man's becoming man, the bearer of intelligence, in the necessities of species and survival. Mutilation is evolution—not easily, not any more humanely than the ogre himself. The ape-like primate is the resurrected boy-man. The polar explorers walk into the teeth of that beginning.

> Things grew worse and worse with us, the old difficulty of breathing came back again and our feet swelled to such an extent that we were obliged to cut open our canvas boots. A form of low fever hung over us. It must be remembered that we were now in the open bay, and in full line of the great ice drift to the great Atlantic, and in boats so frail and unseaworthy as to require constant bailing to keep them afloat.

> The men seemed half crazy; I had not realized how much we were reduced by absolute famine. They ran over the floe crying and laughing, and brandishing their knives. It was not five minutes before every man was sucking his bloody fingers or eating long strips of raw blubber.
>
> Both selections from Elisha Kent Kane.

The true deadly forces with which man must engage are psychic, supernatural, and demonic; they are as present in a meadow as in a badland. In the Arctic, at least this is clear; the outer landscape fulfills inner conditions, and men are compelled to face spiritual and psychological pain as physical pain. This alone makes it bearable.

> Kavik once fell through the ice when it was new in the fall. He swam to solid ice and got up onto it, but found that there was no dry snow in which to roll around to blot the moisture from his clothing. Powdery snow, especially at cold temperatures, effectively absorbs water from wet fur, if it can be reached before the moisture freezes. Kavik took his dogs to shore as fast as he could, and found some soft drifts there to roll in, but it did little good because he had already squeezed out as much of the water as he could and the rest was frozen.

> Kavik was once out on the tundra alone and became lost in a heavy fog. He built a snowblock shelter with a roof and a bench of snow inside. On top of the seat he made a cushion of reindeer moss and sat down on it. He sat in that shelter, which had an open side facing downwind, for four days. Each day he would get up and walk around a little, trying to find a landmark to orient himself, and then he would trace his own trail back to the shelter. He had no food and the only water was that which he melted by putting snow in a tin can held against his body.
>
> Both selections from *Hunters of the Northern Ice* by Richard K. Nelson.

For native Arctic peoples, the conditions are a world map, and an ethnobotany (from which they emerge as shamans, scientists, and healers). Since they are born onto the ice, there is no historical significance to their presence there; it is not even really a badland. The Eskimo migration has been so thoroughly circumpolar, in fact, that they are the one people in the world for whom New World and Old World (North America and Eurasia) are not separated in any cultural or geographical fashion. The interest in their circumstance, from the vantage of this account, is that geographical awareness is coincident with spiritual awareness. Attention to the landscape: the shifting and cracking ice, the disposition of storms and fallen snow, is also meditation and aesthetics. The landscape is an impressive enough encounter that it initiates artists and sorcerors at the same time it teaches geographers and craftsmen.

The one possible book on Moon geography is *Carrying the Fire* by Michael Collins. Collins did not walk on the Moon during the summer of '69, but he flew the command module in lunar orbit while Armstrong and Aldrin were on the surface. The surprising thing about the Collins book is how little of the Moon there is in it. The preparations for the flight far outweigh, in context, the real journey. He describes flying jets at high altitudes, survival practice, a full graduate course in global geology, training in how to assemble and disassemble the space-craft, and even lessons in how to repair the computer at Houston. This is the material Collins internalized, he had to internalize. Unless the mechanics of the flight were known to him at a *deeper* level than the flight required, he would be unable to act in time. Clearly he would not have to disassemble and reassemble the space-craft on the Moon, but by being able to, he could respond with autonomic quickness to its problems. As Collins himself quotes it from his training: "Apollo 8 has 5,600,000 parts and one and one half million systems, subsystems, and assemblies. Even if all functioned with 99.9 percent reliability, we could expect fifty-six hundred defects. . ."

I had an exhange with Nick Dean about this, and he diagnosed very precisely the break that occurs between the Ocean, the Arctic, and the Moon.

> One thing to keep in mind when thinking about Cooper, Melville et al: At the time they wrote, there was still a frontier. Not just in physical or political terms, but that it was still possible, if pressures got too great, to go to sea, to head west, to become a lumberjack.
>
> I think that your description of the number of hours of training required to go to the moon is apt. It removes the possibility of adventure on any but the most vicarious level from most of us. . .
>
> The frontiersman was no intellectual: he didn't have time for it. Our sense of the Frontier (capital eff) is a drawing room product. . .
>
> One reads the log of the "Essex," or Melville. But there is nothing that can adequately describe looking over the rail at Hawke Harbour, Labrador, seeing a roughly hundred-fifty foot steel-hulled catcher vessel sunk in the shallows and KNOWING that she was rammed by a whale and barely made it in. Or standing on the deck of the whaling factory, with the finback pulled up, and the SIDE of the whale towering above me, with

men standing on it, stripping blubber. And at the time, NOT KNOWING that this was nearly the last of it: there was no sense at all of an historical moment.

Collins lacks intimate engagement with the lunar badlands, but he has other insights. For instance, he observes Newtonian mechanics from an extraterrestrial perspective; he SEES night and day for the illusion they are; he has a sharp sense of outer space as medium in which to move; he doesn't forget to tell us that in atmospheric flight one has to speed up to catch an object and in Earth-orbit flight one has to slow down, drop to a smaller swifter orbit, and then rise up, to overtake an object. He is sensitive to relative speeds and motions, and his sighting of the Earth itself speaks directly to an Imago Mundi:

> To actually be 100,000 miles out, to look out four windows and find nothing but black infinity, to finally locate the blue-and-white golf ball in the fifth window, to know how fortunate we are to be able to return to it—all these things are required, in addition to merely gauging its size and color. While the proliferation of photographs constantly reminds us of the earth's dimensions, the photos deceive us as well, for they transfer the emphasis from the ONE earth to the multiplicity of reproduced images.

As for the Moon, there is no doubt that Collins saw it also, but his descriptions are dreamlike and cinematic. They are, in a sense, a more profound description of the machinery in which he is travelling:

> The moon I have known all my life, that two-dimensional, small yellow disk in the sky, has gone away somewhere, to be replaced by the most awesome sphere I have ever seen. To begin with, it is HUGE, completely filling our window. Second, it is three-dimensional. The belly of it bulges out toward us in such a pronounced fashion that I almost feel I can reach out and touch it, while its surface obviously recedes toward the edges...
> Close up, we sped over hill and dale, delighted by its sunny slopes but sobered by its grim and forbidding craters.
> Both are cratered, but the seas do seem calm by comparison with the tortured uplands. The MARIA are darker too and seem more neutral gray than the golden hills which surround them.

The shamanistic tradition, lying outside of Western history, involves a totally different journey to the Moon, re: Carlos Castenada's further dialogues with Don Juan in *Tales of Power*. For similar reasons, the Eskimos considered it an insanity to follow a magnet to the Pole.

> "Last night was the first time that you flew on the wings of your perception. You were still very timid. You ventured only on the band of human perception. A sorceror can use those wings to touch other sensibil-

ities, a crow's for instance, a coyote's, a cricket's, or the order of other worlds in that infinite space."

"Do you mean other planets, don Juan?"

"Certainly. The wings of perception can take us to the most recondite confines of the NAGUAL or to inconceivable worlds of the TONAL."

"Can a sorceror go to the moon, for instance?"

"Of course he can," he replied. "But he wouldn't be able to bring back a bag of rocks, though."

Collins' hallucinatory experience is tied directly to his craft; the following is his first blast-off:

There is absolutely no sensation of speed, and only a moderate increase above one G as we are gently pushed back into our contoured seats. I am dimly aware that a thin overcast layer above us seems to be getting closer when POW we burst through the wispy clouds in brief but clear contradiction to the seat-of-our-pants feeling of standing still. Goddamn, we are moving out!

The whole science fiction sense of rockets and space ships must submit to the speed of the Kwakiutl war canoe in Edward Curtis' movies. That lost space we falsely imagine all this machinery would recover and extend into an infinite so large it could never be lost again: is there canoe after canoe, bear and raven and whale dancing on the prows. They live in wooden houses; the canoes are also wood. There is nothing else. They have no other game. Their space is so limited as to have in it only what is necessary, what *has no* out, as most of this we have gained fails for its billions of problematic pages of newsprint, day after day, making for unlived lives, hence unexperienced voyages and transformations. There may be indigenous Kwakiutl mistakes too, but one thing is certain: their space is total and infinite, and although it includes ocean and land, it also *is* ocean and land. It is the whole that extends in any direction, called once and sometimes "totemic space." As vast as jungle villages and bugs in a rotting log. Witness the ship that roars up from Cape Canaveral, burning off hydrogen and oxygen, shooting toward something that opens continuously wider, planet after planet, the big end of the funnel.

The very water, chemically solvent to life, to protein, washes up onto the beaches, its colors borrowed from plants and shells and from the sky. This is the same thing, however far the other would seem to be extended, as the oars are raised to the point history has taught, and crashed down into the waves, their flat blades throwing the wood forward in a series of continuous lurches, that bear the dancing totem animals to a consecution. The ship flies. As far as the men inside it are concerned, this is the same swiftness as busting through a cloud. The same rush. And they get back the countertension of their bodies causing it, of an energy so great it would seem to warp time and allow them to squeeze through into the ancestral, so much more than the infinite. This, cosmologically, is as large as we could conceive of.

Though we are all men, history surely intercedes in these matters. Your mind is the real computer of that spaceship, even as it is the body that is returned, the only real body that finds the slim entry passage back into the atmosphere: down into the history sea and blue water and salt air just outside your spacecraft, your antiseptic high-jumper limbs—fallen in a heap in a bottle in a jug into the old Greek ocean. The sequence of badlands is tied as clearly to our migratory past as desert and Arctic ethnobotanies are the natural consequence of long habitations. In one sense, the Moon is the reduction of Arctic and Polar exploration; in another sense, it is a different event entirely. The confusion puts cross-hairs right on this spot in Western time.

The City

The city is a badland in some sense we don't quite yet understand. Despite its obvious physical presence, especially in urban decay, the city is an invention solely of intelligence, and if it is not made by man, man is the stand-in for the intelligence that requires it. All physical events in the city are mental: the lights at night, the laws, the design of streets and houses, the museums, the parks. The city is so mental that even sun and wind and electricity come to seem unreal, artificial. Demands can be outrageous, i.e., that a thirty storey building be supplied with heat and water without any raw materials; yet cities appear inexplicably self-sufficient in the imaginations of people growing up in them. If mind could dominate so as to bring all things into being, the eternal city would be realized; we would have a noosphere. But for all its suggestion of a form we do not have, the city is as dependent on the farm for its life as the astronaut is on the support systems of his ship. And the city may share with the prairie its creation by man, but it shares only with the Moon that utopian ephemerality.

The city, which is the tyrant of the original Assyrian-Inca state and the present-day bureaucracy of bad management, is also the polis, the image of Eden, and the celestial city, in which man becomes, without sacrifice and slavery, what he is. A dying polis is more than an abandoned mining town; it is an ancient Phoenician-Egyptian document, standing for something we cannot bear to lose, even as it becomes obscure at the edges. So Olson calls everyone's attention to Winthrop's description of Boston, and the dream that *that city would shine forth from its hills*, containing the whole promise of the New World. Until the imagination can supply that, cities will suffer disorientation and dislocation. In a badland made of mind, greed and malice cannot be hidden in any condition other than the landscape itself.

Standing on that car roof, high above the ground, he felt free. Far off he saw the window of his front room bedroom and the whole wall of tenements. There were stores and people and horses and wagons and trucks. Gino seemed to sail by on an ocean of freight cars—brown, black, yellow, with strange names like Union Pacific, Santa Fe, Pennsylvania. Some empty cattle cars scented the air. Turning, he saw the cliffs of the Jersey Palisades patched with green, and blue water below. Through the hundreds of immobile freight cars a few black round engines chugged quietly, their white smoke adding a fresh burning smell pleasant in the morning summer.   Mario Puzo: *Fortunate Pilgrim.*

What is left. If you return? You deserve to find dead slums. Streets. Yellow houses near the tracks. Someone's mother still dying with an oil lamp. Hillside place.

They would know what to say. Even now. If they weren't afraid. Of myself. Of what I made myself. The blue and orange hills. Red buildings. He wd know, even in the hall, bent over money on the floor. Blues singer. Thin Jimmy with tugged up pegs. Headlight, does that word mean anything to you? Separate persons.

LeRoi Jones: *The System of Dante's Hell.*

The footbridge over Tenth Avenue, no longer needed, had been torn down.

In a few years the western wall of the city would disappear and the people who inhabited it would be scattered like ashes—they whose fathers in Italy had lived in the same village street for a thousand years, whose grandfathers died in the same rooms in which they were born.

Fortunate Pilgrim.

My sister wd be somewhere in shadows pouting, looking down 4 stories at the chinese restaurant, & hump hatted cool daddies idling past in the cold. Snow already past our window quiet on the street. Friday, cool snow, for everyone cd run out new swag coats & slouch towards their breathing lives.   *The System of Dante's Hell.*

Suddenly we were all excited. Dean wanted to tell me everything he knew about Bakersfield as we reached the city limits. He showed me rooming houses where he stayed, railroad hotels, poolhalls, diners, sidings where he jumped off the engine for grapes, Chinese restaurants where he ate, park benches where he met girls, and certain places where he'd done nothing but sit and wait around. Dean's California—wild, sweaty, important, the land of lonely and exiled and eccentric lovers come to forgather like birds, and the land where everybody somehow looked like broken-down handsome, decadent movie actors. "Man, I spent hours on that very chair in front of that drugstore!" He remembered all—every pinochle game, every woman, every sad night.   Jack Kerouac: *On The Road.*

Footnotes

This essay was compiled from notes handed out to my class during a course entitled: "American Literature and Ethnography" (at the University of Maine, Portland, Maine, in the spring of 1972). The notes were updated in 1975 and 1976 with the preparation of this anthology. The "Ocean" section of the original notes was expanded into the essay on Melville's *Whale* when the course changed to a *Moby Dick* seminar.

[1] Cyrus Gordon: *Beyond Columbus.*

[2] Geoffrey Ashe: *Lands to the West.*

[3] For a special section on *The Oak Openings* by James Fenimore Cooper, see *Io*/16, Earth Geography Booklet #4, Anima Mundi; pages 204-256. The contributors include John Morgan, Don Byrd, Russell Gregory, and Karl Pohrt; and there are selections from the Cooper novel itself.

[4] Ursula K. LeGuin: *The Left Hand of Darkness.*

[5] Carl Sauer: *Land and Life.*

[6] For the poem by Fuller, see *Io*/12, Earth Geography Booklet #1, Economics, Technology, and Celestial Influence; page 36.

[7] *Io*/4, Alchemy Issue; page 201.

[8] The sequence on Arctic Regions and the Moon begins in *The Continents* by Richard Grossinger (written in 1969 and published by Black Sparrow in 1973). It continues with: "Mars: A Science Fiction Essay" in the book *Mars: A Science Fiction Vision, Io*/9, 1971; page 175.

[9] For the complete section of Aua's text from which I am quoting, see *Io*/7, Oecology Issue; page 10.

[10] My full essay on this book is called "*The Sea Lions* of James Fenimore Cooper;" it appears in *Martian Homecoming at the All-American Revival Church*, North Atlantic Books, 1974; page 9.

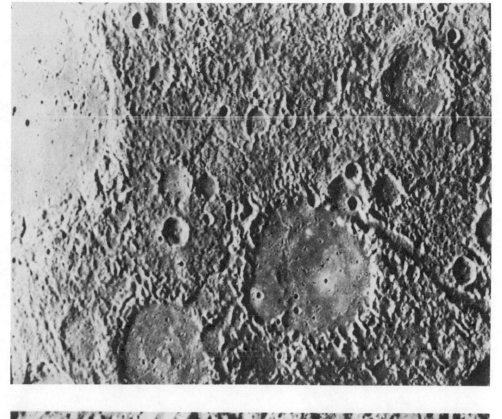

Robin Ridington

Eye on The Wheel

Poem

Only when you come to the place
Where you remember what is happening to you
Will the circle of time
Turn around you
Only when the tracks before you are your own
Will you turn with the circle
When your feet enter the tracks
Of every other being
You will see them as your own
And leave them all
Behind you

Introduction

"Eye on The Wheel" is a myth that begins in the symbols and experience of a nomadic Northern Canadian Indian people, the Dunne-za, and
works its way into the context of our own symbols and experience. If there is
one thing we know for certain about mythic symbols it is that they cannot
be completely pinned down to any particular time and place. The same
symbols, images, messages, relationships, turn up in widely separated loca-
tions in geography and history. The Phoenix appears as shamanic dreamer,
Quetzelcoatl, Pharoah, Christ, and the spark of sentience that always passes
on from generation to generation to reappear changed in form but the same
in essence. The same symbolic patterns return in new foliage, like the seasons, and undergo rapid and regular changes in polarity like the transformation of night into day. As Joseph Campbell, Heinrich Zimmer, Carl Jung,
Mircea Eliade and others have shown, mythic symbols reflect the same
recurring patterns of human experience the world over. To imagine that the
message of a culture's myth relates only to the context of a particular cultural
experience is to deny the possibility of an understanding flowing from one
tradition into another, or of the same understanding emerging independent-
ly in isolated traditions. There is abundant evidence that the same symbolic
patterns emerge from very diverse adaptive conditions. Mythic symbols live,

like the Phoenix, as they enter and re-enter the lives and times of real people.

Although some elements of a story's message may relate particularly to a concern embedded in a particular time and place, without some degree of commonality with our own experience the story would be entirely obscure and untranslatable. A story can be reduced to its logical structure and examined in this anesthetised state by white-coated technicians, but in order to achieve a transformation from one tradition to another it must regenerate itself with new images and messages appropriate to the experience of our lives, here and now. This transformation and regeneration is what has happened to the Dunne-za story told to me by an old medicine person and dreamer named Jumbie. It is a story about the dreamer's vision in a time when the People are in danger.

Among the Dunne-za, children are sent out into the bush on a vision quest where they encounter a giant animal, a monster they already know from the myths they have been told by the old people. In the vision quest they experience the reality of the mythic times when the giant animals hunted and ate people. In the vision quest they begin a transformation from the innocence and dependency of childhood, into the competence and understanding of adulthood. As the Child grows older the meaning of his or her visionary experience comes into focus. The growing Child learns to use this medicine power to focus his dreaming and see the larger pattern of which every small step is only a part. Each medicine animal gives powers and understanding appropriate to its nature. For each medicine animal there is a story telling how the culture hero who travels around the world like the Sun changed the person-eating monster into the animal that is seen in the here and now of everyday reality. A person's medicine power gives him or her the vision to see, from among the many paths that may or may not lie ahead, the clearest path of possibility. Dreaming and vision quest are focal points of Dunne-za culture and experience. In our own culture, neither are institutionalized, but our need to see the larger pattern of which our immediate present is only a part is perhaps even more for us a matter of life and death. For the Dunne-za a small band may be overtaken by starvation but The People as a whole will carry on. But for us, our whole species must face the possibility of its own extinction.

"Eye on The Wheel" begins as a story about the danger an old Dreamer among the Dunne-za sees in the emerging pattern of his dreaming. It is both a story of the danger that lies ahead, out of sight of an ordinary vision focused on everyday reality, and the story of the vision quest experience through which The Dreamer grew into his ability to focus his dreamsight, like an Eagle, on far-away realities. The story then undergoes a transformation from the context of a time and place removed from our own experience to the one in which we live from day to day, unable to see with a dream-sight focused beyond the events of everyday reality until a member of our species first leaves the Planet Earth to look back upon her from his tracks, 240 thousand miles out in space on the surface of the moon. In the alchemy of mythic transformation Neil Armstrong's "giant leap for mankind" becomes a shamanic journey. The two stories of transformative experience merge into one. We come to learn that Dunne-za means simply, "our people, our relatives", and that the monster we feared as children is really one of us in ceremonial mask.

Story told by Jumbie

Once upon a time in April, in late winter, when there were monsters, one old medicine person felt *nagata*, the feeling that something bad was going to happen.

And Robin

The medicine person is a dream traveller, able to leave his tracks in sequential time and ascend to where he can look back on them to see a pattern emerging from the extinguished sunshine of a day that has passed, or has not yet come to pass. His medicine is a song—a trail of song leading up and out of the middle earth to a more perfect one at the centre, beyond the appearance of reality. An old person's trail leads back, step by step, to the experience of a child's vision. Beyond the monster's appearance a child lies quietly in his own time and space waiting for the sun to rise and reveal the trail that lies ahead. The old person has already been over the trail, three days out and three days returning. In either direction, it leads to the time when there were monsters and the monsters are eating the people. Nagata is the dreamer's premonition.

Monsters are eating people. People are becoming monsters. Long ago there used to be monsters on this world. They were driven down beneath the earth's surface. It has been painted over to hide their resting place, but the dreamer, looking back on his trail, remembers them. The white people drill down beneath the earth's surface to get oil from their remains. They use it to make their cars go. A person's trail ends when he steps into one of their cars. To pick it up again the dreamer must go back to confront the monster. The call of his medicine is on the trail behind him. Even when the sunshine has gone he can follow with his mind the trail of song. His heart drum sets the pace, step by step, from there to then, and the ebb and flood of voices washes over the landscape to give it an appearance of reality. For three days you follow the song's turns, up and inside, to the very centre of the emergent pattern. For three days, the trail leads you back to the body you left behind. On the seventh day all connections come together and explode in a burst of light. You cannot go there and you cannot go away from there. At the pattern's centre, old eyes are reflected in those of the child. Together they are the dreamer.

> He felt like that all the time until the time came when the bull moose were getting really fat. Then he and his people moved up the river that comes out of the mountains. They camped three places along the river, past where it turned into the mountains, and they killed a really fat bull moose. Before they hadn't got anything and they were hungry.
> The people who were camped with the old person laughed at him when he said he felt strange. But for six days he felt that way. He couldn't eat because he was afraid. The people just laughed at him. "You won't see any monster," they said, but on the sixth day he said, "Tomorrow the monster will come."

On the seventh day the pattern will come into focus. What had been the uneasy premonition of a dream will materialize in a burst of light, assuming for a time the appearance of reality. The dream tracks before you circle round, like those of a hunter, to come up behind you. Monsters circle round to hunt the people, and consume the appearance of their reality. On the seventh day the dream will appear on the trail behind you. For three days the dreamer follows the trail of his song to the centre; for three days he follows its circle back to the place where his body lies waiting. The monster on your trail will come into focus, in the place where you made your camp three days before. Only when the people see their fear closing with their reality three days before them, will they turn again to see the centre. Perhaps it will then be too late. If anyone knows it will be the dreamer. He has been there and returned. He couldn't eat because he was afraid. The people just laughed at him. Before the child left camp he did not eat because he was afraid. Monsters are eating people. The people are becoming monsters.

> The next day he told the people to move up on top of the high mountain with a flat top. The people moved up there, women and children and the rest. The old person stayed down but then he got really scared and he went up on top of the mountain with the rest of the people, for he had seen something really big where the river turned, where they had camped three days before. That was about thirty miles away. If that thing he saw was little like a moose or a horse he wouldn't have been able to see it from that far away. It was a really big monster and it was following their tracks towards them.
> The Old Person went on top of the mountain and he told the people,

"See, you didn't believe me. Look there and see what is coming." The people went with him and they saw that animal. It had already passed the second place where they had camped. It went fast like a wolverine, and it was huge. It had a white back with two great humps on it. It was *Nowe Nachi*, a giant wolverine. When they saw that the women all started to cry for their babies because they knew that the animal was going to eat them all.

They saw the animal get to their third camp. When they had run away they had left the fire burning, they were in such a hurry. The animal went into their camp. He went to that fire but there was nobody there and he kept on going, right up that mountain after the people, right straight up. The people's tracks went either side but he came on up the steep part.

An Old Person lives in the story of this medicine animal. He wears the mask of its nature as he moves from camp to camp, fire to fire, centre to centre with the people. By these signs they come to know the reality of his dreaming. He is the animal of his story wearing the mask of a human being. His story is real in the space around him. The stories are true for all to see as he moves with the sun through his day and at night, follows the echo of his song, painting the appearance of another reality from the place where the sun will return in its own time. In dreaming the Old Person turns from darkness to the light. With every revolution the pattern of changes comes more clearly into focus. In the quiet time the dreamer is waiting for events to catch up with his vision. The monster will soon be ransacking the camp that was our home and centre only three days before now. In the pattern is the Dreamer's premonition.

Nowe Nachi, giant wolverine, is one of the medicine animals. As an animal he is unlike all the others in intelligence and ferocity. Only Wolverine understands the nature of traps and snares. While other animals struggle to be free, and in their desperate drive for survival take their own lives, Wolverine understands his situation and calmly extricates himself from it. Only Wolverine can go back on his own trail. The others press forward until they are overcome by blackness but *Nowe* sees the light behind him. He knows that the way ahead sometimes lies in the opposite direction. He is the one whose back is painted white. He is the master of traps, able to go back from the illusion of his own reflection. While others strangle in the trap of a reality they cannot be, Wolverine deftly pulls back into the world of possibility. He is master of the feedback signal between existence and possibility. He knows to turn away from where the sun was setting to anticipate its return in the East. To follow the trail of light you must turn to meet it where you know it will return. To follow the trail of your own life you must see the pattern of which each step is only a small part. To turn away from the trap you must know in what direction the path of possibility lies.

When Wolverine breaks into a cache of food the people have stored away he takes what he needs and pisses on what is left. He does not try to live on a place that is dangerous. He leaves his sign, to stop those who would follow in his tracks from taking into themselves the flesh that bears his mark. Monsters are eating people. People are becoming monsters. The dreamer turns to see a giant Wolverine on the trail behind him. Only Wolverine can follow in Wolverine's tracks. Only Wolverine can turn from darkness to the light. Only Wolverine has a white trail painted along the darkness of his body. Only the planet turns, half in darkness, half in light.

When the Human Being became Wolverine he put on his animal mask and pretended to be the victim of Wolverine Man's trap, a pit of pointed stakes painted over to look like an ordinary trail. Only *Nowe*, the Wolverine, can escape the trap by going back over his own trail. Only *Nowe's* song goes back from the blackness to the light. Wolverine Man found him; a blood stained limp bundle at the bottom of the trap. Behind the appearance of darkness there is light. Along the back of his black body there is painted a trail of light, a pit of stakes painted over to look like an ordinary trail. You are going back to *Nowe's* camp in his game bag, a rabbit-sized limp bundle bedraggled in blood. *Nowe* can only escape the trap by going over his own trail from darkness to the light. While others strangle in the trap of a reality they cannot be, *Nowe* deftly pulls back into the world of possibility. You are the child of the monster you turn to meet on your own trail, closing the gap between then and there and here and now. Monsters are eating people. People are becoming monsters.

Wolverine Man says to his kid, "Look, I got a nice fat dude for dinner." You wink at the kid. "Hey Dad, your dude just winked at me." "Like hell he did. I got him from the bottom of the pit, bloody as an afterbirth." You wink again to the kid. Then you jump up and chop the old monster down. Your medicine name is *Nowe*. From that point on wherever you may go the hump-backed monster with the streak of light on his back, a pit of stakes painted over to look like an ordinary trail, will be behind you, coming closer in your dreams, until he becomes the focus of your reality. When game becomes hunter, the monster will be behind you. Only *Nowe* can turn back upon his trail from darkness into light. When the monster is only three camps away from The People you must begin the journey home to where The People are keeping a fire burning for you.

The People have found a way to use energy that comes from there and then. It is a monster growing on the trail behind them. Two hundred Million years ago the sun rose and set, rose and set, over the photosynthetic factories of the Mesozoic. With every turning of her body from darkness into light, the power flowed into the bodies of plants and in them the power remained, through the long gestation that brought about our birth as people. The pipelines reach back two hundred million years. A person's trail ends when he steps into one of their cars. To pick it up again the dreamer must go back to confront the monster. The child is born, limp and bloody, from a pit of stakes. People are becoming monsters. You wink at the kid in the mirror. Then you jump up and chop the old monster down.

People are living from energy that overbalances their understanding of it. No one dreamed that the Sun of the Mesozoic would return, but now it is only three days camp from where we are. When the feedback signal between what you have and what you need becomes too far removed from your experience of what is real, you begin eating up parts of your body before you realize what you are doing. Even to have begun as we did was to have gone too far. The Eye on The Wheel is too far from both brain and ocean to bring them both around to a common centre. Looking back, the pattern that emerges is clear from the tracks of the embryo, but when we were high on the wave of energy there was only the desire of here and now to rush along with it. Your back was turned when *Nowe* winked at the kid, but you remembered it as you grew into understanding. Only when the energy is nearly gone is the message finally delivered. In a story the Medicine person turned into a child. In time the child grew into a medicine person. The pain of touching fire keeps the child safe from its burning. The feedback is instantaneous. The pain of living high off a Mesozoic credit card will not withdraw the body to the path of possibility in time for all to find their way back along the trail.

The children who grew into the understanding of their age will follow an old person's trail back, step by step, to the experience of a child's vision. The reality of here and now is painted to look like an ordinary trail over a pit of stakes. The People are moving forward together toward darkness. They are animals struggling to be free and in their desperate drive for survival they are taking their own lives. The medicine person is feeling that something bad is going to happen, but The People cannot yet feel the pain of their loss.

Trap makers are flying through the atmosphere, high on 200 million year old Sun power reading Time magazine. They are flying into an unacknowledged pattern at the centre beyond the appearance of their reality. The species is flying to the common centre where Brain and Ocean are in balance. The child looks back to remember his emergence, limp and bloody from a pit of stakes. Look back. Look back. Cretaceous, Jurassic, Triassic, Permian, Carboniferous. They are a parabolic time mirror, concentrating the energy into a laser beam burning painlessly through the vital organs. The trail leads three days out of the edge of the possible universe, and three days back to where the planet body spins in waiting before birth and after death. On the seventh day the monster will return as a child, but no-one will believe it. When the people have run as far as they can go they will turn to *Nowe*. The monster has been eating The People for a long time. He has been taking their tracks into his machines and blasting them far and away from their here and their now. Only The Dreamer can go back to where the tracks rejoin the path of possibility. Only the dreamer can see by the light of his song when the appearance of reality is darkness.

> The Dreamer took off his clothes and wrapped himself in a pure white moosehide and he went down the mountain to that giant animal. When the old person was pretty close he called out to the animal "Where the hell do you thing you are going?". The animal didn't see him. He looked back to where he was coming from. The Old Person met the animal and he put his hand on the animals chest and he said, "Stop!". The animal looked at him and said, "You're the one I am looking for." That old person knew that animal from when he was a child. "Follow me down the river," he said, and the giant animal went back where he came from.

The Dreamer's body rotates on its axis once a day and circles around The Primary once a year. When the tracks before you are your own, you will turn with the circle and leave them all behind you. You are the one I am looking for.

The Dreamer left his body rooted in the Earth and turned to face the monster in his tracks. It was the body of a child whose tracks were pressing on to the place where the trail would have to cross a pit of stakes, painted over to give the appearance of reality. In his hand The Child holds a toy plastic space ship. "One small step for man; one giant leap for Mankind." In 200 million years the tracks of Neil Armstrong will still be fresh and clear on the lifeless body whose rotation perfectly matches her own revolution. It is two hundrd and forty thousand miles from sea to shining sea; one is the ocean that received the first spark and grew you in embryo; the other, a sea of lifeless tranquility, able only to reflect the spark but not to receive the seed.

Two Hundred Million Years ago the tracks of dinosaurs led them to extinction, but the energy of their age has jolted us out of our body's familiar orbit into the pattern of an unfamiliar dream. "It involves a technology so complex no one person can understand how to master it all. 20 thousand contractors; 20 million pages of manuals, instructions and other material printed monthly by the Kennedy Space Center alone". The trail ahead has the appearance of reality. "The rocket and spacecraft encompass more than five million separate parts; the engines, the most powerful in the world, gulp 15 tons of kerosene and liquid oxygen a second and get five inches to the gallon." The child's toy plastic space ship is real. The sight of a living planet rising from the rim of her satellite sky mirror is real. The trail to extinction is also real in its possibility.

The species has gotten itself into a high risk occupation. Neil Armstrong said, "I have been in relatively high risk businesses all my adult life. Few of the others, however, had the possibility of direct gains in knowledge which this one has. I have confidence in the equipment, the planning, the training. I suspect that on a risk-gain ratio, this project would compare very, very favorably with those to which I've been accustomed in the last 20 years". (Neil Armstrong, Toronto Globe and Mail, July 21, 1969). In 200 million years the tracks of Neil Armstrong will still be fresh and clear on the reflecting body with no biosphere, 240 thousand miles from the nearest moving ocean. What life-forms then will swim and swarm inviting spaces? The dinosaurs may know, but they can only say to us, "15 tons of kerosene and liquid oxygen a second, five inches to the gallon, 240 thousand miles out from the ocean of birth and 200 million years into lifeless tranquility." On a risk-gain ratio only the dreamer knows how this project would compare with those to which you have been accustomed in the last 200 million years.

"The dreamer wrapped himself in a pure white moosehide and went down the mountain to that giant animal." The dinosaurs did not look ahead to see their own extinction. The Child with his toy plastic space ship cannot see to the extinction of his reality. "Where the Hell do you think we are going?" Both Dreamer and Child look back along their tracks. The future of the species depends upon the reality to which the Child has been accustomed for the last 20 years. The Dreamer can see the child's reality in the embryo's coded memory, but the Child cannot see The Dreamer moving from the world of possibility into his reality. The child holds onto the appearance of his reality, a toy plastic space ship made of mesozoic hydrocarbons, but the Dreamer has long since let it go. "Stop!" You cannot come to where I am and you cannot go away from our common time and space. The Child holds on while The Seed is letting go. The moment of reality is Here and Now. Put down your Time Magazine and turn to see the reflection of possibility in a Dream. I am the one you have been looking for. At the end of his trail, the Old Person, wearing a pure white moosehide, turns to meet the monster. It is a Child holding tightly a toy plastic space ship. Face to Face, Mind to Mind, Planet to Planet, Experience to Experience, Image to Reflection, all connections come together and explode in a burst of light beyond illusion. The message from the Mesozoic is a feedback signal between experience and possibility.

"In eons to come, should astronauts from the deeps of space—from other solar systems in other galaxies—pass this way, they may find our spoor, our abandoned gear. A plaque of aluminum affixed to the deserted LM descent stage portrays the two hemispheres of our planet; upon it are engraved the name of our space ship, the date of our mission and a roster of the crew. From these data, the equipment, and even the dimensions of our footprints, intelligent beings will readily deduce what kind of creatures we were and whence we came. We leave a piece of fauna—a falcon feather—and of flora—a four-leaf clover." (David R. Scott, Apollo 15 Commander)

While others strangle in the trap of a reality that cannot be, the Dreamer deftly pulls you back into the world of possibility. He is dreaming of the One Child, cradled in a nest of Frankincense and Myrrh. You are The Child of the monster you turn to meet on your own trail coming together face to face, experience to experience, to close the gap between then and there, and here and now. You are flying back to the nest of life, the blue-green biosphere, flowing along the dreamer's trail down to the river of water painted over the low places, inclining in a single direction down to an ancient understanding Ocean of Time and Space. "Follow me down the river," he said, and the giant animal went back where he came from. Follow the river down to the Ocean Mother, weeping salt tears of Joy at your birth and transformation. Follow the mesozoic hydrocarbons back, inclining in a single direction to a flash of sunshine, on the surface of the ocean of then and there. Follow the tracks of the dinosaurs, down past the darkness of their extinction, to become a toy plastic space ship landing, with less than 20 seconds of mesozoic hydrocarbon fuel remaining on the dust strewn, impact-etched, basalt filled, three thousand five hundred thousand million years old, lifeless, sea of tranquility shimmering into focus out of the ages. The Eagle has landed. "That's one small step for a man, one giant leap for Mankind." The last frontier has become a lifeless world able only to reflect the seed but not to nourish it. The Eagle has been given the gift of reflective vision, looking back on his nest of frankincense and myrrh from 240 thousand miles away.

In a dream, the child Neil Armstrong could, by holding his breath, hover over the ground. (Toronto, Globe and Mail, July 21, 1969). In 200 million years his footprints will continue to walk upon The Sea of Tranquility, his rotation perfectly matching his own revolution. From the Eagle's perspective, intelligent beings will readily deduce what kind of creatures we are, and whither we are going. The Man must labour step by step from one extremity of his life to another, but the Dreamer within him can hover above the ground by holding his breath, take a giant leap to enter the tracks of every other being, and leave them all behind him. The Child is holding on at the same time The Seed is letting go.

Follow me up to the flowing river trail inclining in a single direction up to an ancient understanding ocean of time and space. Where is the giant animal when he has gone back to where he came from? Intelligent beings will know from the tracks he leaves behind. One of the monster's small steps is a giant leap for mankind. A day is when his body rotates once on its axis. A year is when it circles once around The Primary. A life is when he meets a point of transformation, and returns to carry on in different form. Looking back, the pattern that emerges from the dreaming is clear from the tracks of The Embryo. Follow them back to the moment of joining and the body is a sphere, touched by a seed on the sea of the Mother. While the Child holds onto a toy plastic space ship the seed is letting go. The giant animal is a sphere spinning once a day and circling round The Primary once a year. Turn to meet the body's image and see yourself reflected in her living reality. You cannot go there and you cannot go away from there.

> The people moved back to their camps. The old person was still wearing his moosehide and he told them he was going out to meet the monster. He said he wouldn't be gone very long, and he went out. Not too far away he met that big animal. He was gone four days and the people began to worry about him. They thought something had happened to him.

You were a child when you first encountered the monster. The camp to which you returned on the Seventh Day has long since passed into memory, but you have lived on to become the Old Person who sent you alone to the edge of your Child's world. Now you must return to recover the Child's remains in the camp of your memory. "Tranquility base here; The Eagle has landed". When you turn to meet the giant on the trail behind you, it will be a little Child. In a dream The Child Neil Armstrong is holding on to the breath of a distant earth, hovering above his tracks wanting more than anything to fly away on a trail of song. In your embryo a tadpole is swimming, gill breathing the ocean of 200 million years ago. His breath hisses through the regulator, hisses through his pursed voice strings singing the moment of return, hisses through the transformations of modality and frequency to penetrate the 240 thousand miles of emptiness to where we wait in suspended animation before the swimming picture tube images hissing breathlessly before us. "Tranquility base here; The Seed has landed the The Embryo is letting go. I'm going to step off the LM now. That's one small step for a man; one giant leap for mankind." The Child who held his breath for 39 years, 11 months, 2 weeks and 2 days, has finally come down to a different world. His breath releases in the words that fly across the emptiness to reach our minds.

> The surface is fine and powdery. I can, I can pick it up loosely with my toe. It does adhere in fine layers like powdered charcoal to the sole and sides of my boots, I only go in a small fraction of an inch, maybe an eighth of an inch, but I can see the footprints of my boots and the treads in the fine sandy particles. Beneath the treads I can feel the thin crust of a reality that moves with my tracks through sequential time. What has

79

passed never goes away but it will change constantly as we ourselves change. There seems to be no difficulty in moving around. As we suspected, it's even perhaps easier than the simulations at 1/6 G that we performed on the ground. Its meaning is determined by our understanding of its place within a completed circle. If we would be free of the shadows lurking in our tracks we must turn to face them. It's actually no trouble to walk around. The shadows are the dark reflections of ourselves as we might have been. They are the fear of darkness behind us. To follow the trail of light you must turn to meet it where you know it will return. We're essentially on a very level place here. It's quite dark here in the shadow, and a little hard for me to see that I have good footing. The People's trail begins when a person steps out of the Child's toy plastic space ship and come together in a burst of light. It has a stark beauty all its own, much like the High Desert of the United States of Concentration and Release. It's different but it's very pretty here. Here Men from The Planet Earth first set foot upon The Moon, July, 1969, A.D. Here The People turn to illuminate the shadow world behind us. Here the Child walks in tracks we laid down before him. Out of the many have come a single destiny, "E Pluribus Unum".[1]

You wink at the Child and read the rest of the plaque. "We Came In Peace For All Mankind".

> The Old Person went back to the camp. His old old father was named Tsuketa, Father of Tsuke. He knew that animal too; he knew it better. The old person, his child, didn't want to follow that animal, but his father told him he should go. "You should go. He will make you a strong medicine person. It's good medicine." So his child went after the monster.
>
> The old person-child went out to meet that animal. He stayed with him seven days and the animal showed him every kind of trick. The monster slept on top of him. On the seventh day the monster told him to go back. He knew that Tsuketa was worrying about his child. He told him, "If you go a little way from here you will meet your father."

A sleeping past covers the appearance of your reality receeding into blackness in every direction. Only the Dreamer can see by the light of his song, when the appearance of reality is darkness. Even when the mesozoic sunshine is gone you can follow with your mind the trail of song. The spinning planet's heart-drum sets the pace, the ebb and flood of seasons stepping one after another over the intervening ocean of time. The language of its resonance and harmonic connection with what you already know from experience leads you on, with the appearance of reality. For three days

[1] Some of the words of this quotation were actually uttered by Neil Armstrong (National Geographic, 1969). But they have been adapted for my purpose, and I have added to them words which I feel would have been appropriate for Amstrong to say, but which he did not.

80

you follow its feedback signal inside to the very centre of the vanishing and reappearing pattern. For three days you will have to follow your own tracks back toward a new beginning. On the Seventh Day the pattern comes into focus. Breath is released, becomes vibration, becomes sound, becomes meaning, becomes reality, becomes past, and passes on in waves to dissipate on the shoreless immensity beyond. Waves become song, become pathway, become master of the feedback signal between experience and possibility. If you go a little way from here, you will meet the living shadow of the seed from which you grew, nourished in a blue-green biosphere scented with the gifts of frankincense and myrrh. The Seed is dreaming of his Child, The Species of our Embryo 200 million years ago.

Before you return to join the planet of your birth, seed for the coming generations, listen to the voice of the monster crackling through the earphones of your toy plastic space ship. Intelligent beings will be able to deduce even from the dimensions of his footprints what kind of creature he is and where he came from.

> The monster told Tsuke, for that was the old person's name, "I am going to meet your *saze* (sister's child)." Tsuke's saze knew the monster too. He too was old but he had known him when he was young. The monster said, "His mouth stinks too much. He doesn't have much power now." He said that the relative would go out hunting but he wouldn't see him, even when he was close. Then Tsuke went back a little way and met his father. "You're still alive," his father said, and Tsuke said, "Yes". They went back to camp together.
>
> Tsuke's saze went out hunting the next day. He saw the tracks of the great big monster and he started following them. All day he followed those tracks. He saw that they were coming from where his relatives were camped and he thought that the monster must have eaten all of them. But it soon got dark and still he hadn't seen the monster so he went back to his camp. He told the people, "All day I followed the tracks of *Onli nachi*, but I couldn't catch up with him. Maybe he didn't want me to see him. His tracks were coming from where my relatives camped. Maybe he ate them all. That's how the story goes. That is the end of the story.

Wolverine is seldom seen even when he is close to you. The Child wishes to believe in the reality of every possibility; the Old Person only in what he has experienced. Look back to when his tracks were last on the surface of another reality. Look back to the feedback signal from the mesozoic. With less than 20 seconds of fuel remaining, Eagle has landed on the tranquility of three thousand five hundred thousand million years, without transformation in the appearance of its reality. Eagle has landed at the bottom of the pit of stakes painted over with an image of reality. The trap baited with a rabbit-sized limp bundle, bloody as an afterbirth. To bring the Eagle down the hunter lies in a pit beneath the surface of the earth and covers his body with blood. When the Eagle has landed, the hunter must grasp it with his bare hands and take its life bloodlessly by cutting off his breath. From the Old Person's story we know that the Child whose tracks lead back to *Nowe Nachi* must grow up to become Eagle hunter, baiting the trap with an image of his own earth embryo. Take from Eagle his breath of wind, the sound of feathers holding on to air, and letting air pass him by. Take from the highest flier the trackless path of his song. Follow it to where he lives, a nest of frankincense and myrrh, a sweetly scented biosphere.

"There is a certain bird which is called a Phoenix. This is the only one of its kind and lives 500 years. And when the time of its dissolution draws near, that it must die it builds itself a nest of frankincense and myrrh, and other spices, into which, when the time is fulfilled, it enters and dies. But as the flesh decays a certain kind of worm is produced which, being nourished by the juices of the dead bird, bring forth feathers." (Early Christian Father Clement in *Secret Teachings of the Ages*). A Falcon feather and a four leaf clover. When the Child rises as Eagle he is painted with the rainbow colours. Only The Dreamer's vision can know how this project would compare with those to which you have been accustomed in the last 200 million years. Only The Dreamer remembers the trail before him as a place he has been before. Only the dream traveller leaves his tracks on this world to take up ones on another. Only The Dreamer sees his body 240 thousand miles away, supported by a thin crust of reality. Only The Dreamer sees mesozoic sunshine in his toy plastic space ship. Only The Dreamer sees the path of possible reentry into a life-sustaining biosphere. The trail of song is coming from the centre of where The People are camped. The monster's trail leads to the centre of the planet's body. A fire is burning in the centre of camp. The people are singing and dancing, the sound of their voices together passing up with the smoke. When he saw that the monster's trail was coming from where his relatives camped he thought that the monster had eaten them all. All day he followed the tracks of the monster but could never catch up, even with his shadow. Within the dark generation of her dream-shrouded body, the Ovum rotates once a day, and circles round The Primary once a year. You are a drop of seed falling home from one dream into another, a drop of clouded earth falling through space, a drop of sentience reflected on the motionless sea of tranquility. You are person, ape, monkey, lemur, shrew, lizard, salamander, fish, worm, egg, growing in a nest of frankincense and myrrh. You are growing feathers, catching your breath, painting the visible spectrum in a circle around your moment in time and space, turning to meet The People on the path of possibility. All energies revolve around a single point of light. All darkness is where the light is unseen. You cannot go there and you cannot go away from there. In the quiet time the Dreamer is waiting for events to catch up with his vision. His eye is on the wheel.

82

Russell Gregory

For a Sacred Bundle

1.

This small carving's a Polar Bear,
made from ivory, a walrus tusk:
for you at ending of a year.

2.

He lives on ice, in icy seas,
floe to floe, miles from land,
swimming strongly.
                He covers
his black nose with a paw to hunt,
the People say,
          or Seal would see
him coming.
         Our largest carnivore—
in size, not deadly appetite:
we have him there,
            ton by megaton.

3.

Bear suffers our Pisan pride
for up to thirty years:
we foul him with our eyes
until his fur is urine-yellow.
Cages are no way to life,
even if one were mad;
& sanity's another lie agreed upon
—like zoos on Sunday afternoons,
a bearskin on polished parquet floor.

4.

Pursued on his hunting grounds—
you can see his tracks four-hundred feet up—
Bear rears
     & snarls
          at loaded planes;

one buzzes,
                    banks
                          & softly lands—
on bloodied snow:
                          death from above
would be mythical & right—
if we were even vaguely godlike.

                    5.

Dead in snow,
                    on film,
                                    in photograph,
Bear supports superb suburban boots,
a British rifle,
a German scope—
custom-made to yield a sporting death:
"dominant predators of the Arctic,"
the classy guide-book smoothly says.
The pelt, tanned & combed,
deodorized & mothproofed,
decorates a panelled wealthy wall,
"between my Elk & Mountain Buck."
Man's the animal who whines his end;
Bear & others live & answer as best
they can
          —& disappear;
& we are all a little more extinct.

                    6.

Not many Polar Bears survive.
This carving totems a dying race—
to bring you dreams
                    & give you power:
riding floes is how to live—
feast your own sweet dangers
but beware the yellow-eyed beast
who guns
          for Bear
                    & you
                          alike.

7.

Like Bear, raise your arms to greet
the sun:
            for what we praise—
beyond
            above
                        around
                                    out there—
has to come home & say itself as love
or Bear's death would be no crime,
your love no hurt to live or leave.

19.xii.1972

James Bogan

Ptolemy Meets the Pharoah

for Denise Low

——"Sound is faster than light."

I'm sittin on a rough-cut wood bench (curve of buzz saw signature sweeps across the plank). The bench is supported by the floor of a 70 year old house whose foundation is set in the Ozark Plateau which has been above water now for 300 million revolutions of the Earth about the Sun. I raise my head, look up and out feeling that Sun's heat on my face. It is noon, Sun-time. Beyond the Sun is Aquarius, which I cannot see, for the 10 mile thick veil of blue betwixt us.

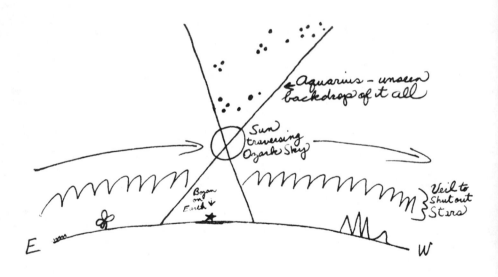

Pharoah Sanders plays
"Sun in Aquarius"
to celebrate the occasion.

Dark transition
from Capricorn:
Lonnie Smith delving
into piano
thrumming
the taut strings
like a subterranean harp—
fearful sound of temple guardians
at the threshold
scarin off demons
dis/speling miseries
before the door
that opens swiftly to
sweet flight
wheeling and delight
of saxophone and liquid voice
bells
      drums
            flute
                and
                    drums

Bass duet
funky spinal talk

Consumed in
acceleration
of glowing saxophone
screamin and wailin
into the Sun
propelled by
lung/compression
heart/fire
fuel of transmuted pain
ground in low resonance
of droning chimes:

"Accept and cleanse
this offering."

And a return
to oh so easy
dancin
and yodeling, even.

"Father and Mother,
I return from flames of fire
tried and pure and bright."

Not exhausted
but revitalized
in fission/fusion
breeder reaction
freeing soul/energy
in purifying intensity.

Entropy confounded.

January 25, 1975
Rolla, Missouri

Ishmael Reed

from Flight to Canada

PART I
Naughty Harriet

Flight to Canada

Dear Massa Swille:
     What it was?
     I have done my Liza Leap
     & am safe in the arms
     of Canada, so
     Ain't no use your Slave
     Catchers waitin on me
     At Trailways
     I won't be there

     I flew in non-stop
     Jumbo jet this a.m. Had
     Champagne
     Compliments of the Cap'n
     Who announced that a
     Runaway negro was on the
     Plane. Passengers came up
     And shook my hand
     & within 10 min. I had
     Signed up for 3 anti-slavery
     Lectures. Remind me to get an
     Agent

        Traveling in style
     Beats craning your neck after
     The North Star and hiding in
     Bushes anytime, Massa
     Besides, your negro dogs
     Of Hays & Allen stock can't
     Fly

By now I s'pose that
Yellow Judas Cato done tole
You that I have snuck back to
The plantation 3 maybe 4 times
Since I left the first time

Last visit I slept in
Your bed and sampled your
Cellar. Had your prime
Quadroon give me
She-Bear. Yes, yes

You was away at a
Slave auction at Ryan's Mart
In Charleston & so I knowed
You wouldn't mind
Did you have a nice trip, Massa?

I borrowed your cotton money
To pay for my ticket & to get
Me started in this place called
Saskatchewan Brrrrrrr!
It's cold up here but least
Nobody is collaring hobbling gagging
Handcuffing yoking chaining & thumbscrewing
You like you is they hobby horse

The Mistress Ms. Lady
Gived me the combination
To your safe, don't blame
The feeble old soul, Cap'n
I tole her you needed some
More money to shop with &
You sent me from Charleston
To get it. Don't worry
Your employees won't miss
It & I accept it as a
Down payment on my back
Wages

I must close now
Massa, by the time you gets

This letter old Sam will have
Probably took you to the
Deep Six
That was rat poison I left
In your Old Crow

Your boy
Quickskill

1

Little did I know when I wrote the poem, "Flight to Canada," that there were so many secrets locked inside its world. It was more of a reading than a writing. Everything it said seems to have caught up with me. Other things are running away. The black in my hair is running away. The bad spirits who were in me left a long time ago. The devil who was catching up with me is slipping behind and losing ground. What a war it was!

Lincoln. Harriet Beecher Stowe. Douglass. Jeff Davis and Lee. Me, 40s, and Stray Leechfield. Robin and Judy. Princess Quaw Quaw Tralaralara. Mammy Barracuda. Cato the Graffado. Yankee Jack. Pompey. Bangalang. It affected us all one way or the other.

"So you're the little woman who started the big war," Lincoln was supposed to have said. Received Harriet Beecher Stowe in the White House only to have her repay his courtesy by spreading the rumor that he was illiterate. They were always spreading rumors about Lincoln. That he and his son Todd were drunks. That Mrs. Lincoln was mad. That he was a womanizer. That his mother Nancy Hanks was a slut. The Confederates said that he was a "nigger." Who is to say what is fact and what is fiction?

Old Harriet. Naughty Harriet. Accusing Lord Byron of Cornography. She couldn't take to Lincoln. She liked Nobility. Curious. The woman who was credited with ruining the Planters was a toady to Nobility just as they were. Strange, history. Complicated, too. It will always be a mystery, history. New disclosures are as bizarre as the most bizarre fantasy.

Harriet caught some of it. She popularized the American novel and introduced it to Europe. Uncle Tom's Cabin. Writing is strange, though. That story caught up with her. The story she "borrowed" from Josiah Henson. Harriet only wanted enough money to buy a silk dress. The paper mills ground day and night. She'd read Josiah Henson's book. That Harriet was alert. The Life of Josiah Henson, Formerly a Slave. *Seventy-seven pages long. It was short, but it was his. It was all he had. His story. A man's story is his gris-gris you know. Taking his story is like taking his gris-gris. The* thing that is himself. It's like robbing a man of his Etheric Double. People pine away. It baffles the Doctors the way some people pine away for no reason. For no reason? Somebody has made off with their Etheric Double, has crept into the hideout of themselves and taken all they found there. Human shells walk the streets of the cities, their eyes hollow, the spirit gone out of them. Somebody has taken their story.

Josiah Henson went away and fell in love with wood. Nobody could take his wood. His walnut boards. He took his walnut boards to England and exhibited them at the Crystal Palace. Met the young Queen Victoria.

Nobody could take away his Dawn, his settlement in Canada.

Harriet gave Josiah credit in her The Key to Uncle Tom's Cabin. What was the key to her Cabin? Strange woman, that Harriet. Josiah would never have thought of waging a plot-toting suit against her. Couldn't afford one anyway. Besides, he was bad at figures. His Dawn went broke because he was trusting and bad at figures. It's unfortunate when a man's Dawn goes broke, leaving him hopeless and frustrated. When I see those two men in The New York Times in a booth in a fancy restaurant—two bulb-faced jaded men, sitting there, rich as Creole Candy, discussing the money they're going to make from the musical version of Uncle Tom's Cabin, and they have those appetizers in front of them and three kinds of wine—when I see that, and when I see their agent in National Era swimming in the ocean with his Chow dog, I wonder why won't the spirits go out to Long Island and touch him. Touch him for what he did to Josiah Henson. Touch him like they touched Harriet.

Harriet paid. Oh yes, Harriet paid. When you take a man's story, a story that doesn't belong to you, that story will get you. Harriet made enough money on someone else's plot to buy thousands of silk dresses and a beautiful home, "One of those spacious frame mansions of bland and hospitable mien which the New England joiners knew so well how to build." A Virginia Plantation in New England.

Henson had to sell Dawn, his settlement, to pay his creditors. Is there no sympathy in Nature? Dawn, that's a pretty name. Are people lost because the gods have deserted when they said they never would? They promised they never would. Are they concealing themselves to spite the mean-minded, who are too unimaginative to recognize the new forms they've given themselves? Are they rebuking us for our stupidity? They are mean and demanding. They want to be fed. But before you can feed you have to recognize. They told Josiah Henson to behave with "gentlemanly dignity." But the common people knew. Guede knew. Guede is here. Guede is in New Orleans. Guede got people to write parodies and minstrel shows about Harriet. How she made all that money. Black money. That's what they called it. The money stained her hands.

When Lord Byron came out of the grave to get her, the cartoon showed Harriet leaving her dirty stains all over Byron's immaculate and idealized white statue. Did Josiah Henson do this? The man so identified with Uncle Tom that his home in Dresden, Canada, is called Uncle Tom's Museum? Did Tom have the power the Brazilians say he has? Does he know "roots"? Umbanda. Pretos Velhos, Pai Tomas, Pai Tomas. The "curer." Did Tom make Byron's ghost rise out of his undead burial place of Romance and strangle Harriet's reputation, so that one biographer entitled a chapter dealing with the scandal "Catastrophe?" Do the old African and Indian gods walk the land as the old one said they would, too proud to reveal themselves to the mean-minded? The mean-minded who won't pay attention. Too hard-headed and mean-minded to see. Harriet's HooDoo book. "I was an instrument of the Lord," she said. HooDoo writing.

Do the lords still talk? Do the lords still walk? Are they writing this book? Will they go out to Long Island and touch these men who were musing in the restaurant about the money they were going to make on the musical comedy Uncle Tom's Cabin? *Will they get the old mummy grip?*

Harriet said that Byron was fucking his sister. She said that she'd gotten it from her friend Lady Byron whom she felt had been slandered by Countess Guiccioli, Byron's last mistress and the tramp of the Tuilleries Gardens. Harriet accused Byron and his half-sister Augusta Leigh of sharing lustful embrace. Is that why Harriet, the spinster, referred to Lord Byron as a "brilliant seductive genius?" Watch what you put down on the page, Harriet. Did Harriet want to trade places with Augusta Leigh and transform Byron into her brother, Henry? History sure is complicated, or can you, like Stray Leechfield, cash your way out of history?

Why isn't Edgar Allen Poe recognized as the principal biographer of that strange war? Fiction, you say? Where does fact begin and fiction leave off? Why does the perfectly rational, in its own time, often sound like mumbo-jumbo? Where did it leave off for Poe, prophet of a civilization buried alive where, according to witnesses, people were often whipped for no reason. No reason? Will we ever know since there are so few traces left of the civilization the planters called "the fairest civilization the sun ever shone upon," and the slaves called "Satan's Kingdom. Poe got it all down. Poe says more in a few stories than all of the volumes by historians. Volumes about that war. The Civil War. The Spirit War. Douglass, Tubman, and Bibb all believing in omens, consulting conjure and carrying unseen amulets on their persons. Lincoln, the American Christ, who died on Good Friday. Harriet saying that God wrote Uncle Tom's Cabin. *Which God? Some gods will mount any horse. Even the spinster school teacher crawling like an animal from the sightseeing bus toward an Umbanda temple with no a priori beliefs, as they say.*

Dressed in white planter's pants, white waistcoat, and white shoes, Raven Quickskill dines alone at the end of a long white Virginia table.

He has just dined on a good old Southern meal of plum pudding, wild duck, oyster soup, and Madeira wine, the kind of meal Kentucky Generals used to sup at Jeff Davis' "white house" in Montgomery before the South was reduced to corn bread and molasses. All of the boarders had left the Castle for the weekend. All fifty of them. Craftsmen from all over the South, blacksmiths, teachers, sculptors, writers. Uncle Robin became exultant when Quickskill made the suggestion. He couldn't figure his way out of his inheritance. He and Judy travelled a lot. Now they were in the Ashanti Holy Land. Their last trip out they had brought back some serpents. They had given Quickskill the whole first floor of their castle. It was airy and had big spacious rooms. Mountains, meadows, and the Atlantic Ocean could be seen through the windows. Quickskill would write Uncle Robin's story in such a way that, using a process the old curers used, to lay hands on the story would be lethal to the thief. That way his Uncle Robin would have the protection that Uncle Tom (Josiah Henson) didn't. (Or did he merely use another technique to avenge his story? Breathing life into Byron.)

Raven has the Richmond newspaper spread out in front of him. Princess Quaw Quaw has been arrested carrying a fifteen-foot balance pole, two American flags at each end, while walking on the steel cables of the Golden Gate Bridge. In the photo, crowds were hurling pellets at the officers for interfering with Quaw Quaw's act. She was beginning to become an international event, and the media speculated about her every action. She was becoming the female Blondin, a characterization she resented. "Why don't they call him the male Quaw Quaw Tralaralara?" she once protested in an interview.

This is not to say that she became a media bug. She insited on her privacy and occasionally there were photos of her wandering about her husband's yacht, nude, wearing sun glasses, as he docked off Trinidad, Mallorca or Sausalito.

The note she had left Quickskill on the dresser of the Eagle Hotel had read merely "Gone South" with her signature scrawled underneath.

He had sent a note to her in care of her agent:

Dear Quaw Quaw Wherever or Whoever:

Maybe one day people of your class will realize that people of my class must grovel, worm, and root our way through life fending off the bad birds so we've little time to take those we love under our wing. And that we become like mythical Goofus birds, invented by lumbermen I think, who fly backwards and build their nests upside down. We get smashed and our endings are swift.

And she wrote back:

Dear Raven:
   And I thought our people were bad, worshipping Bears, Turtles, Ravens, Coyotes and Eagles, but your people worship any old thing or make an "object of reverence" of just about any "new things," as in that HooDoo expression you once taught me, "Only Ghosts Hate New Things," and then that morning I saw you, in our berth, on the steamer, Lake Erie mumbling before it, the typewriter was sitting there and seemed to be crouched like a black frog with white clatter. You thought I was asleep.
   And it went on that way until one day she signed a letter, "See you soon." And that was that. She'd be back. She always came back. And then they'd be back to back. They always had quarrels about "the human condition" as her Columbia Professors would say.
   "Flight to Canada" was the problem. It made him famous but had also tracked him down. It had pointed to where he, 40s and Stray Leechfield were hiding. It was their bloodhound, this poem "Flight to Canada." It had tracked him down just as his name had. The name his mother gave him before she went away into the Fog Woman. It had dogged him. "Evil Dogs Us." Yes, indeed. His poem flew just as his name had flown. Raven. A scavenger to some, a bringer of new light to others. The one who makes war against the Imonooks of this world. As quick on his opponents as a schooner on a slaver. "Flight to Canada" had given him enough mint to live on until he did Robin's book. "Flight to Canada" had taken him all the way to the White House where he shook hands with Abe the Player, as history would call him, and hobnobbed with Walt Whitman.
   He had never gotten along with Uncle Robin in slavery, but away from slavery they were the best of friends. He would try to live up to the confidence Robin had in him by writing a good book. "You put witchery on the word," Robin said. He would try to put witchery on the word.
   Uncle Robin had turned down an offer from Jewett and Company of Boston's best known writer and had put his story in the hands of Quickskill; "Now you be careful with my story," Robin said. "Treat that story as precious as old Swille treated his whips." They both knew what that meant.
   Bangalang came into the room from the kitchen. She was about to leave to return to the Frederick Douglass Houses where she and her husband lived. His carriage was outside waiting for her.
   "Is there anything else I can get for you?" she asked Quickskill.
   "No," he said and then, "Bangalang?"
   "Yes, Quickskill?"
   She had gotten a little grey. They had all gotten a little grey.

"Do you hear from Mammy Barracuda and Cato the Graffado?"

"Last I heard, she sang before the last reunion of Confederate Soldiers. They....."

"What happened, Bangalang?" She'd begun to laugh.

"She sang a chorus from 'Dixie.' Well, I have to tell you when she got to those lines that go 'Will run away - Missus took a decline, oh / Her face was de color ob bacon-rin-oh!,' the old soldiers took her to their shoulders and marched her out of the convention hall. Cato was leading the parade like a cheerleader, I'm telling you. Well, if you need something else, there's an apple pie in the kitchen." She turned and walked out.

Curious. Even in the Confederate anthem there was a belle fading away and losing her color. What was this fascination with declining belles in the South? What was the South all about? I'll have to include all of this in my story, Quickskill thought.

Quickskill drank his coffee. He had a swell. His belly was up again. He spent so much time in thought, he forgot about his stomach. That was the writing business all right. He'd been writing since he could remember; his "Flight to Canada" was to him what blacks were to old Abe.

"Abe Lincoln's last card or Rouge et Noir" was the caption under the wood engraving printed in *Punch* magazine. It showed Lincoln beating a Confederate with his ace of spades. Inside the card's black spade was the grinning Negro. The engraving was by Sir Johgn Tenniel, a Royalist. He'd have to write all of this in Robin's story. Raven was the first one of Swille's slaves to read, the first to write, and the first to run away. Master Hugh, the bane of Frederick Douglass, said, "If you give a nigger an inch he'll take an ell. If you teach him how to read, he'll want to know how to write. And this accomplished, he'll be running away with himself."

Master Hugh could have taught Harriet Beecher Stowe a thing or two.

Richard Grossinger

Melville's Whale: A Brief Guide to the Text

I. Melville Criticism

A— Twentieth Century Academic Perspectives on Melville:
Social Idealism and Naturalism

Moby Dick is a book rediscovered in our present intention of completing history. The disperse interpretations of it are the attempts of different modern schools to claim it as a predecessor in their own orthodox traditions. Famously, the pseudo-epigraphic replaces the prophetic, and holy books become the symbolic histories of an expansionist modern age.

My own prejudice is to place Melville in a lineage that includes Cooper, Poe, Emerson, Whitman, the authors of the Bureau of American Ethnography monographs, Pound, Sauer, Williams, and Olson (with gestures toward Celia Thaxter, Willa Cather, Francis Parkman, James Audobon, James Malin, etc.). In "Equal, That Is, To The Real Itself," Olson mentions the "unhappy thought that Melville can be put at the head of a literary use which includes Twain, Dreiser, Hemingway, and Faulkner," a use which implies Melville was concerned primarily with humanism, naturalism, and democracy, i.e., the *Pequod* symbolic of America, with a representative black, an Indian, some lower class rabble, and Ahab the tyrant, who spawns social upheaval and sinks the ship (of potential democracy). "As if this is what Herman did it all for," Olson says on the Goddard tape.[1]

My own knowledge of this tradition is hearsay, plus what I remember from high school and college English courses and what I take from Olson's essay (in which a particular author, Milton R. Stern, is *demolished* for his book *The Fine Hammered Steel of Herman Melville*).[2] Stern, if I understand him in Olson's translation, is part of the Eastern academic establishlment (that is now getting its clock cleaned by Imamu Baraka on the one side as effectively as the fiscal conservatives on the other, while it continues to grow off the waning fat of the land). Their social idealism is tied to an outmoded and unfounded empiricism, with an unacknowledged stake in coaxing Newtonian laws into social physics where reasonable and humane men, acting pragmatically, create a just society. Although Melville could hardly be pushing this, a desire to find it has made its own sect. In the postscript to the Harper and Row paperback edition of *Moby Dick*, Jerry Allen argues: "To be left out anywhere in life, to be forced by circumstances or monomania into isolation from his fellow beings, was, to Melville, the supreme calamity for man. It is this thought that permeates *Moby Dick*."[3] This of a man who valued his own monomania over all ameliorations and considered polite egalitarianism the supreme calamity of the human spirit. The only possible excuse for such a misreading is that the academics fear so much what Melville *is* saying they assume he is being sociological and ironic, i.e., he is saying exactly the opposite. This is the only way he gains entry to the club founded in his name. But god knows Melville was not a liberal and not a do-good reformer.

And then naturalism: which Olson diagnoses as another version of materialism, separating creation from artistic process by posing nature as a finished drama. In the words of Jerry Allen: "[*Moby Dick*] celebrates man's primeval struggle with nature depicted in terms of American nineteenth-century whaling, and in its richly complex symbolism, it questions man's very concepts of good and evil." To call the event Ahab shares with Moby Dick a "primeval struggle with nature" is lazy cosmology. Melville did not have that famous misunderstanding that we're what *we* are and then *nature* is something else out there. As Lévi-Strauss writes in *The Raw and the Cooked*, culture is, after all, simply the social condition of natural things; his jaguar is kin to Melville's whale (and hardly someone you can avoid having to dinner by the same rules that made Melville's marriage for him too). After all, Ahab's mind is as much nature as Moby Dick's body (or Moby Dick's mind and Ahab's body). And where is the struggle? Melville emphasizes again and again the persistence of an event, without once reducing it to a dichotomy of foes. "Good and evil" are simply part of an inherited text Melville mocks in a pretence of adoption.

> The jaguar and the man are polar opposites, and the contrast between them is doubly formulated in ordinary language: one eats raw meat, the other cooked meat; in particular, the jaguar eats man, but man does not eat the jaguar. The contrast is not merely absolute: it implies that between the two opposite poles there exists a relation based on a total absence of reciprocity.[4]

On the other hand the jaguar is the discoverer and guardian of fire; the jaguar clan, mythologically made up of real jaguars, is the only source of new marriage partners. Fire, so useful in cooking, in making men not jaguars, is a marriage gift of wild jaguars who precede, ontologically, every instance of a jaguar clan.

> In order that all man's present possessions (which the jaguar has now lost) may come to him from the jaguar (who employed them formerly when man was without them), there must be some agent capable of establishing a relation between them: this is where the jaguar's (human) wife fits in.[5]

As he appears in Indian literature, the jaguar is a paradoxical beast:

source of culinary habits and civilization, but only as a civilized being who has reverted totally to nature, abandoning his ungrateful in-laws, who continue, in that strange but accurate mythological injustice, to enjoy the fruits of his labor. His jaguar characteristics, over which he now has no control, are violated semantically, in the jaguar clan and the tales of its origin. The Indian who successfully evades the jaguar of the jungle finds that he or she has married one. At the same time that culture attempts to gain its freedom from nature, by strong prescriptions and taboos, their inevitable inconsistency returns customs to the wilder condition in which they originated. The whale can neither be rescued as a fellow mammal nor abandoned in the fury and malevolence of the hunt. Melville seeks him as the Bororo seek the jaguar, as both a historical-etymological object at the beginnings of civilization and an irrational outlaw on the *boundaries* of civilization. He is as easily a source of oil as a solution to a riddle.

So, if we are going to have a struggle, we can do a little better than man against whale.

B— Olson and Lawrence

Melville couldn't abuse object as symbol does by depreciating it in favor of subject. Or let image lose its relational force by transferring its occurrence as allegory does. He was already aware of the complementarity of each of two pairs of how we know and present the real—image & object, and action & subject—both of which have paid off so decisively since. "Equal, That Is, To The Real Itself."

The whale towers above most animals of American nineteenth century literature: raw and totem, nervous, territorial, subject to cosmic rhythms. If the book appears symbolic or allegorical, it is not because Melville loaded it but because shape is continuous and connection inevitable. In D'arcy Thompson's *On Growth and Form*, we are told, very specifically, that the bend in the conch *is* the horns of the ram, *is* music, and water splashing. If the whale's condition gives rise to others, so it is with all animate and phenomenal things, in the overall confluence and harmony of creation.

Congruence was spatial intuition to Kant, and if I am right that Melville did possess its powers, he had them by his birth, from his time of the world, locally America. As it developed in his century, congruence, which had been the measure of the space a solid fills in two of its positions, became a point-by-point mapping power of such flexibility that anything which stays the same, no matter where it goes and into whatever varying conditions (it can suffer deformation), it can be followed, and, if it is art, led, including, what is so important to prose, such physical quantities as velocity, force and field strength.[2]

Yet my high school copy of *Moby Dick* is filled with attested symbols. In the chapter "The Lee Shore" I copied from class lecture:

> shore = safety, peace, conventional religion in which one is told what to think, Christianity. The ship is the soul of man. The wind is society and convention. The water is independent thought. To reach heaven one must stay away from conventional religion.

The chapter, as written, is lucid. Any fisherman could read it. Wind is atmospheric, not societal. A ship is very ordinary and very complete. If it seems to be symbolism (and it does), this is Melville's playful truancy (as with good and evil) in making a heathenish visit to the church he no longer attends.

Some people prefer *Moby Dick* in the abridged version, with only the adventure story and allegory; college courses liberally omit chapters on whaling and whales. This is actually a more prejudicial reading of the book than the straight technical chapters would be. The parts are not, as they might be in Dickens or Cooper, simply commensurate aspects of a complex linear narrative. They are equations developing at different . .ogical levels. When fragmented, they are exponentially reduced.

Much contemporary art has this noncommutative quality, especially those works with a structural or conceptual bias. This does not make *Moby Dick* the forerunner of cubism or jazz; Melville's legitimate sources are still native and Biblical; his whale shares more with Haida totem sculptures than the forms of Marisol or Oldenburg. In our half of the twentieth century, topological and syntactic awareness is a birthright of artists, and they borrow from microscopes, radio-telescopes, and computers the way Melville borrowed from Keats and Shakespeare and Plato. But:

> We inherit a complex mass of unapprehended mental attitudes which go back not only to Greece and Rome, not only to Ur and Memphis, but back beyond this to the hunters and fishers of the Ice Ages. What we like to call our thinking may be as much conditioned by the fears and prejudices of the mammoth-hunter or the Neolithic peasant as by the religious aspirations of the early Semites or the speculative thought of the Greeks. Our ancestry not only includes Plato and the New Testament, but the sweaty blood-stained ritual of Stone Age magic, and the irrational terrors of the world of shaman and seer.   Stuart Piggot in *Ancient Europe*.

To which Olson adds, in the Goddard lecture:

> . . . like EVERYTHING was really in existence, in powerful ways, back before Alexander. Don't be fooled by the universalization of the present. The work, the real work, of the future has already been done, and the future that is proposed for us is a lie.[6]

The roughness Olson discerns in Melville is pre-Greek and non-Euclidean (the Ugandan of the *Maximus*),[7] and not that later scientific overthrow of Euclid (though I suspect these are finally the same in all other senses but the one in which I am discussing them, and Melville's accuracy was in making the archaic original seem like the postmodern). Whereas Keats and Shelley revived the classical metaphorically and in terms of bounded poetics, Melville touched *Gilgamesh* and *The Dead Sea Scrolls*. His whale is more Tiamat than Leviathan, and his religion is Uranus, Baal, Astarte, Yahweh. Ahab *is* King Ahab, not King James. The discontinuous spaces in *Moby Dick* are the actual discontinuities of the transmission, the roughness is the static: gods who are, at the same time, stars and societal conditions, stretched across gulfs so wide their bodies are not only almos⁻ broken, they are broken, and this is how we receive them today. The Romantic cannot confront the "Processural." In this Melville comes to say:

> By visible truth we mean the apprehension of the absolute condition
> of present things.

So Olson refers not to Melville's knowledge but his inheritance of the forms he used, a blind and intuitive inheritance, and no doubt Lawrence was thinking of *The Whale* when he wrote:

> The furthest frenzies of French modernism or futurism have not yet reached the pitch of extreme consciousness that Poe, Melville, Hawthorne, Whitman reached. The European moderns are all *trying* to be extreme. The great Americans I mention just were it. Which is why the world has funked them, and funks them today.
> *Studies in Classic American Literature.*

The ambiguity of *Moby Dick* lies in a mystery Melville never clarified, even in the living of it. It is like those Dionysiac mysteries to which Aeschylus confessed (that he was ignorant) in order to save his life (all the time not knowing whether he had stumbled upon them, in his ignorance, or not).

II. Melville's Supernatural

A— The Elemental

Melville's nature went beyond a natural realm. Or, if nothing is beyond, he charted those zones of the phenomenal universe that naturalists evade, the paradoxes of matter and motion. He was no sea-painter or bullfighter, and his Pacific is no cousin to Twain's Mississippi. To hell with the scenic and sympathetic: he had big clues: to vibration, polarity, and field. With Plotinus and Blake, he was the author of a visionary physics yet unborn. (Tyranny and democracy, good and evil: these are Madison Avenue abstractions in the sense that the whole academic world is a product and

101

source of Madison Avenue, but the current classroom versions are sold under these catchy logos.)

Nature, for Melville, was but the knowable fabric of creation, the spare visible space in which the intrusions of the unknowable occur. In this sense, he has as little to do with Hemingway as Yogananda with Philip Roth. Even as he implicitly rejected the social physics of American liberalism and rah-rah democracy, he picked the precise hole in Newton, in the closed and accountable systems of events. He shared with Poe a hidden world to which even our traditional occult is a bare surface scratching. But he was more observant than Poe, a better hermeticist; he read appearances sharply and rarely played idle metaphysics because he could do it with a storm at sea. For Melville the natural was itself supernatural, and the so-called super-natural simply a decorative and derivative evasion. Where Poe takes up with mesmerism, Melville describes the spinal column and flukes of the whale. Who would question that these are equally strange manifestations of an unknown power. Spooks and emanations are obvious, but the ribs and vertebrae of the whale, by their particular embodiment and relentless preci-sion, their resemblance to things known and their location in things con-cealed, are truly terrifying. The whale need not be ghost to be entity. If there is a demon pursuing us, he is concealed *with* us in creation. The moment of contact is that contact is never broken.

> All the trees, with all their laden branches; all the shrubs, and ferns, and grasses; the message-carrying air; all these unceasingly were active. Through the lacings of the leaves, the great sun seemed a flying shuttle weaving the unwearied verdure. Oh, busy weaver! unseen weaver!—pause!—one word!—whither flows the fabric? what palace may it deck? wherefore all these ceaseless toilings? Speak, weaver!—stay they hand!—but one single word from thee! Nay—the shuttle flies—the figures float from forth the loom; the freshet-rushing carpet for ever slides away. The weaver-god, he weaves; and by that weaving is he deafened, that he hears no mortal voice; and by that humming, we, too, who look on the loom are deafened; and only when we escape it shall we hear the thou-sand voices that speak through it.   "A Bower in the Arsacides."

B— The Malign

If *The Whale* is not an account of man against nature, there is still a foe, one who, Melville says, in a passage we shall come to, has as little to do with nature as it does with man.

> Consider the subtleness of the sea; how its most dreaded creatures glide under water, unapparent for the most part, and treacherously hid-den beneath the loveliest tints of azure. Consider also the devilish brilli-ance and beauty of many of its most remorseless tribes, as the dainty

embellished shape of many species of shark. Consider, once more, the universal cannibalism of the sea; all whose creatures prey upon each other, carrying on eternal war since the world began.   "Brit."

To Melville's eyes, the brilliance and beauty of the remorseless tribes seem to go beyond, in the tantalizing face it present to us, natural necessity and the diversity necessary for survival ("only seems to," Darwin would say). "Then why such stunning camouflage?" the Melvillians reply. And if Darwin answers: "Sexual recognition," they laugh at his innocence: since when did Satan ever need such an excuse.

The whale is hardly Melville's "life form of the month." It operates "as that unexampled, intelligent malignity," calculating and committed. Where the followers of Darwin will later see whorls of mutation and gene drift and the wondrous complexity of life, the Melvillians see malevolence and trickery. Coming from a totally different place, Melville predicts the current psychology of mammal behavior and auras: the whale is intelligent, its intelligence is of a different order than man; where man goes, he attracts disembodied intelligence. If Melville fails latter-day ecological consciousness, it is not because he lacks sympathy for the whale, as we shall see. It is because the magical world and the natural world have become hopelessly entangled, and like Confucius, he is finally more bound by the ceremony than the lamb.

> Genius in the Sperm Whale? Has the Sperm Whale ever written a book, spoken a speech? No, his great genius is declared in his doing nothing particular to prove it. It is moreover declared in his pyramidical silence.   "The Prairie."

On the one hand, the whale is historically Egyptian, linked to the hieroglyphs as ancient human text; on the other hand, it is magical and Luciferian, in touch with the human world only blindly, and as part of some alien design. Its kinship, as a living sentient form, is with the voices and allies Castaneda speaks of (through Don Juan) in his books on initiation. Whale or mushroom, wind or shadow, crow or moth, natural as their appearances may seem, in the flood of world phenomena, they are not things themselves, or themselves alone. As entities, they use the available and manifold bodies of the incarnated sphere.

> The White Whale swam before him as the monomaniac incarnation of all those malicious agencies which some deep men feel eating in them, till they are left living on with half a heart and half a lung. That intangible malignity which has been from the beginning; to whose dominion even the modern Christians ascribe one-half of the worlds; which the ancient Ophites of the east reverenced in their statue devil;—Ahab did not fall down and worship it like them; but deliriously transferring its idea to the

abhorred White Whale, he pitted himself, all mutilated, against it. All that most maddens and torments; all that stirs up the lees of things; all truth with malice in it; all that cracks the sinews and cakes the brain; all the subtle demonism of life and thought; all evil, to crazy Ahab, were visibly personified, and made practically assailable in Moby Dick.

"Moby Dick."

There is a flash here of the "devil's chemistry" of Gnostic and Zoroastrian sources (from which light and darkness battle right down to the electron, in the modern version, and beyond: where we know not, except that they come again and again, despite destruction, to life). And then there is the part that comes from somewhere else entirely, as it is dispatched into this world:

THE PYRAMIDS loom, a long slope of crags and precipices; the tablerock overhanging, adhering solely by mortar, twisted at angles like broken cliffs. Masonry—and is it man's? The lines of stone do not seem like courses of masonry, but like strata of rocks. Slanting up the sweeping flanks people move like mules on the Andes. They ascend guided by Arabs in flowing white mantles, conducted as by angels. These are the steps Jacob lay at.

I shudder at the idea of the ancient Egyptians. It was in these pyramids that the idea of Jehovah was born. A terrible mixture of the cunning and the awful. Moses was learned in all the lore of the Egyptians.

No wall, no roof. In other buildings, however vast, the eye is gradually innured to the sense of magnitude, by passing from part to part. But here there is no stay or stage. It is all or nothing. It is not the sense of height or breadth or length or depth that is stirred. It is the sense of immensity that is stirred.

The theory that they were built as a defense against the desert is absurd. They might have been created with the Creation.

As with the ocean, you learn as much of its vastness by the first five minutes' glance as you would in a month, so with the pyramid.

Its simplicity confounds you. Finding it vain to take in the sea's vastness man has taken to sounding it and weighing its density; so with the pyramid, he measures the base and computes the size of individual stones. It refuses to be studied or adequately comprehended. It still looms in my imagination, dim and indefinite.

The tearing away of the casing, though it removed enough stone to build a walled-town, has not one whit subtracted from the apparent magnitude. It has had just the contrary effect. When the pyramid presented a smooth plane, it must have lost as much in impressiveness as the

ocean does when unfurrowed. A dead calm of masonry. But now the
ridges majestically diversify.

It has been said in panegyric of some extraordinary works of man,
that they affect the imagination like the works of Nature. But the pyramid affects one in neither way exactly. Man seems to have had as little to
do with it as nature.   *Melville's Journals.*

Hints of *Chariots of the Gods.* As though these stoneworks were de-
posited by intergalactic travellers. Hints of Crowley. As though they are the
remains of magical circles and the invocations within them.

"Vengeance on a dumb brute!" cried Starbuck, "that simply smote
thee from blindest instinct! Madness! To be enraged with a dumb thing,
Captain Ahab, seems blasphemous."

But the connection of hieroglyph and pyramid and whale is initial. It is
a magical war. And who could believe otherwise than that Ahab speaks also
for Melville.

"Hark ye yet again,—the little lower layer. All visible objects, man,
are but as pasteboard masks. But in each event—in the living act, the
undoubted deed—there, some unknown but still reasoning thing puts
forth the mouldings of its features from behind the unreasoning mask. If
man will strike, strike through the mask! How can the prisoner reach
outside except by thrusting through the wall? To me, the white whale is
that wall, shoved near to me. Sometimes I think there's naught beyond.
But 'tis enough. He tasks me; he heaps me; I see in him outrageous
strength, with an inscrutable malice sinewing it. That inscrutable thing is
chiefly what I hate; and be the white whale agent, or be the white whale
principal, I will wreak that hate upon him. Talk not to me of blaphemy,
man; I'd strike the sun if it insulted me."   "The Quarter-Deck."

"...seems to have as little to do with it as nature..."
This is a Persian sun, an ancient Paleolithic sun Ahab has fallen upon in
vision. And:

... Moby Dick had reaped away Ahab's leg, as a mower a blade of
grass in the field. No turbaned Turk, no hired Venetian or Malay, could
have smote him with more seeming malice.   "Moby Dick."

It could only be gnostic magic, unless we prefer a ledger-book of economics or "the old man and the sea."

...here thou beholdest even in a dumb brute, the instinct of the
knowledge of the demonism in the world. Though thousands of miles
from Oregon, still when he smells that savage musk, the rending, goring
buffalo herds are as present to the desert wild foal of the prairies, which
this instant they may be trampling into dust.

Thus, then, the muffled rollings of a milky sea; the bleak rustlings of the festooned frosts of mountains; the desolate shiftings of the windrowed snows of the prairies; all these, to Ishmael are as the shaking of that buffalo robe to the frightened colt!

Though neither knows where lie the nameless things of which the mystic sign gives forth such hints; yet with me, as with the cold, somewhere those things must exist. Though in many of its aspects this visible world seems formed in love, the invisible spheres were formed in fright.

"The Whiteness of the Whale."

We will never know why Melville believes this. Nor does *Moby Dick* even begin to tell. It was not only the nightmare of the pagan Pacific, but the nightmare that the Pacific awakened in him. This never was a safe world.

For Herman, man is without adequate cosmology, and the war is for creation itself. Those who see it only as an attack on the church miss that it is an attack on both the church and science, their twin origin in the Greek, their joint cowardice and bluff, their rank inability (despite hardy premises) to shield man from the forces he must go up against, their failure to launch even the semblance of a counterattack. He mocks and blasphemes them not in triumph but in sorrow, sorrow for the ease of his own conversion in the Pacific, among pagans—that *their* magic was no more but no less effective. Western man has been tricked by technology and medicine into an illusion of protection.

Then gazing at his quadrant, and handling, one after the other, its numerous cabalistical contrivances, he pondered again, and muttered, "Foolish toy! babies' plaything of haughty admirals, and commodores, and captains; the world brags of thee, of thy cunning and might; but what after all canst thou do, but tell the poor, pitiful point, where thou thyself happenest to be on this wide planet, and the hand that holds thee: no! not one jot more! Thou canst not tell where one drop of water or one grain of sand will be tomorrow noon; and yet with thy impotence thou insultest the sun! Science! Curse thee, thou vain toy, and cursed be all the things that cast man's eyes aloft to that heaven, whose live vividness but scorches him, as these old eyes are even now scorched with thy light, O sun! Level by nature to this earth's horizon are the glances of man's eyes; not shot from the crown of his head, as if God had meant him to gaze on his firmament. Curse thee, thou quadrant!" dashing it to the deck, "no longer will I guide my earthly way by thee; the level ship's compass, and the level dead-reckoning, by log and by line; *these* shall conduct me, and show me my place on the sea... "The Quadrant."

And, from quantum physics, Heisenberg writes to the same point:

In a darkened world no long illuminated by the light of [the] center,

106

the 'unum, bonum, verum'... are scarcely more than despairing attempts to make Hell a more agreeable place to live in . This must be particularly emphasized against those who think that by spreading the civilization of science and technology even to the uttermost ends of the earth, they can furnish all the essential preconditions for a golden age. One cannot escape the Devil so easily as that.[8]

In abandoning the quadrant, Ahab not only abandons science but the whole society that has brought it into being, plus the illusion that something real is being measured, something more than the inertial structure of the device itself. And god knows, our whole world today lies upon such an uncertain and vain needle.

Even to the death, Ahab and Melville retain a profound sorrow for the port that is lost, the haven they long to retreat to, an act which Starbuck, like the minister in his Sunday sermon, thinks is, not exactly easy, but at least a matter of will—but for which *they* have no methodology.

> Oh, immortal infancy, and innocency of the azure! Invisible winged creatures that frolic all round us! Sweet childhood of air and sky! how oblivious were ye of old Ahab's close-coiled woe! But so have I seen little Miriam and Martha, laughing-eyed elves, heedlessly gambol around their old sire; sporting with the circle of singed locks which grew on the marge of that burnt-out crater of his brain...
>
> "Oh, Starbuck! it is a mild, mild wind, and a mild looking sky. On such a day—very much such a sweetness as this—I struck my first whale—a boy-harpooner of eighteen! Forty—forty—forty— years ago!— ago! Forty years of continual whaling! forty years of privation, and peril, and storm-time! forty years on the pitiless sea! for forty years has Ahab forsaken the peaceful land, for forty years to make war on the horrors of the deep!...
>
> From beneath his slouched hat Ahab dropped a tear into the sea; nor did all the Pacific contain such wealth as that one drop.
>
> "The Symphony."

Ahab and Melville reject the pastoral and gentle not because they do not adore it but because they are commissioned otherwise. To spurn that commission would leave them hounded as Jonah by God. The world of his family and children is lost to Ahab even as the domestic is lost to Melville in his room upstairs writing it, recalling De Quincey's opium dreams, in which he is held a prisoner by demons while his children play within earshot. The dim echo of a graceful loving world is always in the background, and, in this age anyway, we believe in cures instead, perhaps because a grimness of magical and political obsession is so unrelieved.

Starbuck and the others are unwilling accomplices. Ahab drags them in because he requires them, like the animals and novitiates Crowley exploits

107

in his ceremonies. Starbuck, like benevolent capitalism, invokes the share-holders, the investors, the widows and children. This is why the liberals are so in love with him. He is *their* delegate to the *Pequod*. He is against a war that protects investments he (like them) doesn't even know he has.

Malignity, as all magic, uses money and bodies for its own purposes. When *Moby Dick* becomes a ritual book, Fedallah replaces Starbuck. He is not humane or ethical. But Starbuck cannot be Ahab's aide-de-camp, and Turkey, with its military government and opium fields, as even Henry Kissinger affirms, is an invaluable ally. His agelessness and non-human credentials make him a career participant in the war (once oil is cast aside and the *Pequod* sails into the circle). No wonder businessmen are gun-shy of missions and crusades, unless, as in Astrodome conversions, the mission itself becomes the business. You can't deal with someone who's got nothing to lose.

> A pale, death-glimmer lit up Fedallah's sunken eyes; a hideous mo-tion gnawed his mouth.
> Like noiseless nautilus shells, their light prows sped through the sea; but only slowly they neared the foe. As they neared him, the ocean grew still more smooth; seemed drawing a carpet over its waves; seemed a noon-meadow, so serenely it spread. At length the breathless hunter came so nigh his seemingly unsuspecting prey, that his entire hump was dis-tinctly visible, sliding along the sea as if an isolated thing, and continually set in a revolving ring of the finest, fleecy, greenish foam. He saw the vast, involved wrinkles of the slightly projecting head beyond. Before it, far out on the soft Turkish-rugged waters, went the glistening white shadow from his broad, milky forehead, a musical rippling playfully accompanying the shade; and behind, the blue waters interchangeably flowed over into the moving valley of his steady wake; and on either hand bright bubbles arose and danced by his side. But these were broken again by the light toes of hundreds of gay fowl softly feathering the sea, alter-nate with their fitful flight; and like to some flag-staff rising from the painted hull of an argosy, the tall but shattered pole of a recent lance projected from the White Whale's back; and at intervals one of the cloud of soft-toed fowls hovering, and to and fro skimming like a canopy over the fish, silently perched and rocked on this pole, the long tail feathers streaming like pennons.   "The Chase—First Day."

This is the altar.

And when Ahab is sacrificed to his own experiment, we can assume that, someday, Ahab returns, elsewhere more likely than here, with leg-aches and vague traumatic memories.

Or is Melville Ahab reborn (his vertigo and remote terror, recalling a battle from the Mediterranean or Black Sea). It wasn't a whale. It was Tiamat, or some other entity. It was not loss of limb at sea but lameness from a disease contracted in mountain passes under Oriental rain, recalling an inherited lameness. Melville creates Ahab neither out of sympathy nor outrage, but: "My life is a memory beyond birth." If not reincarnative, then the overall trace we bear of this whole thing happening in another place in another way.

> Yes, there is death in this business of whaling—a speechlessly quick chaotic bundling of a man into Eternity. But what then? Methinks we have hugely mistaken this matter of Life and Death. Methinks that what they call my shadow here on earth is my true substance. Methinks that in looking at things spiritual, we are too much like oysters observing the sun through the water, and thinking that thick water the thinnest of air. Methinks my body is but the lees of my better being. In fact take my body who will, take it I say, it is not me. And therefore three cheers for Nantucket, and come a stove boat and stove body when they will, for stave my soul Jove himself cannot.   "The Chapel."

The whale-hunt is hardly some foolish sporting battle; it is fought by men already scarred beyond any possibility of manhood or humanity. Melville is closer to Dante than we are to him. Literally:

> Ha! a coward wind that strikes stark naked men, but will not stand to receive a single blow. Even Ahab is a braver thing—a nobler thing than *that*. Would now the wind but had a body; but all the things that most exasperate and outrage mortal man, all these things are bodiless, but only bodiless as objects, not as agents.   "The Chase—Third Day."

Mark Twain my ass. Does this not put Mr. Melville directly with H. Rider Haggard and the Edgar Allen Poe of "Mesmeric Revelations" and "Eureka?":

> In this sense, of course, *perfection of plot* is really, or practically, unattainable—but only because it is a finite intelligence that constructs. The plots of God are perfect. The Universe is a plot of God.
> And now we have reached a point at which the intellect is forced, again, to struggle against its propensity for analogical inference—against its monomaniac grasping at the infinite. Moons have been seen *revolving* about planets; planets about stars; and the poetical instinct of humanity— its instinct of the symmetrical, if the symmetry be but a symmetry of surface: —this *instinct*, which the Soul, not only of Man but of all created beings, took up, in the beginning, from the *geometrical* basis of the Universal irradiation—impels us to the fancy of an endless extension of this system of *cycles*.   "Eureka."

And Melville himself on mesmer:

> It was my turn to stand at the foremast-head; and with my shoulders leaning against the slackened royal shrouds, to and fro I idly swayed in

what seemed an enchanted air. No resolution could withstand it; in that dreamy mood losing all consciousness, at last my soul went out of my body; though my body still continued to stay as a pendulum will, long after the power which first moved it is withdrawn.

"Stubb Kills a Whale."

Yes, two occultists, two novice magicians, but also two nineteenth century scientists struggling a bare inch before Planck, before Einstein, Heisenberg, and Kirlian.

III. *Typee*, *Mardi*, and *Pierre:* A Sequence Around *Moby Dick*

A— Ethnography (*Typee*)

Melville's first book, *Typee*, is a realistic adventure story about being captured by cannibals in the Pacific after deserting ship. It has only the barest hint of an initiation. He lived among aborigines and never once let out the secret, so hard it is to know from the text that Fayaway was his lover and mother of his children. *Typee* is pastoral and ethnographic; Herman of the book returns to America and wants to be accepted as a citizen (a hundred years later he would be an anthropologist presenting his work to NIH for a post-doctoral grant). The futility of this flight becomes all the more apparent when one realizes that even *Typee* disturbed people, and was rejected by most as a fiction and a romance.

Moby Dick has no explicit totemic geometries or Marquesan cosmology, but it also has no pastoral illusions. Herman doesn't have the patience anymore. He has worn out his civility and his ease. He doesn't "peep at Polynesian life" (the subtitle of *Typee*). He doesn't say: "Here I am, an American among cannibals; isn't this strange?" The initiation is silently over, and so is the confession of heresy.

Moby Dick arises in a pagan and demonic world, not even pre-Christian, in the trappings of a whaling voyage. Somewhere between *Typee* and *The Whale* Melville has changed, dramatically even from *Mardi*. The Marquesan vision may once have been a traveller's tale with which to charm friends during long winter evenings (as Ishmael telling "The Town-Ho's Story" at The Golden Inn in Lima). Now, in the delayed awakening, he is freed from the promised trauma only so long as he writes the book, which explains the whirlwind in which he put it down and the surety he felt afterwards. He knew what they wanted from him, and he knew they kept their part of the bargain while he was writing it (from whom he had thought to escape by boat only to find himself back again). He knew he must have been writing *their* book, their deep Pacific oblique backwards-over-the-Earth vision of the movement of the shadow, America its fleeting ghost.

The whole possibility of *Moby Dick* lies in its dictation, its integrity as a rough draft of a more eloquent text. That's where Hawthorne missed: he thought Melville should have written the lighter book.

> Whence come you, Hawthorne? By what right do you drink from my flagon of life? And when I put it to my lips—lo there are yours & not mine. I feel that the Godhead is broken up like the bread at the Supper, and that we are the pieces. Hence this infinite fraternity of feeling. You did not care a penny for the book. But now & then as you read, you understood the pervading thought tht impelled the book—and that you praised. Was it no so? You are archangel enough to despise the imperfect body, and embrace the soul. Once you hugged the ugly Socrates because you saw the flame in the mouth and heard the rushing of the demon, —the familiar,—and recognized the sound; for you have heard it in your own solitudes.   Melville to Hawthorne.

Melville precedes Castaneda in that same thing: What happens to Western man once outside his Western experience?... if he is strong enough to return from the abyss? (And if it is a more evident sorcery in Castaneda, it is because our literal and science fiction age requires exaggerated disclosures of the most obvious things).

The true events of *Typee* slowly corroded in the soul of Herman, where they were transformed, hermetically, into the materials of *Moby Dick*. It may be false psychohistory to suggest that Melville was a bearer of radical forms because he touched them in their pagan origin in archipelago, but it does suggest the profound merger of two streams: the totemic space of the Pacific and the beginnings of non-linear topology in Euro-American science.

B— Cosmology (*Mardi*)

Mardi is where *Moby Dick* was almost written. Not enough deepening yet, the broth too pale.

"We are off!" Melville writes. Not: "Call me Ishmael." But the rhythmic impulse is there.

> We are off! The course and topsails are set; the coral-hung anchor swings from the bow; and together the three royals are given to the breeze that follows us out to sea like the baying of a hound. Out spreads the canvas—alow, aloft—boom-stretched on both sides with many a stun' sail, till like a hawk, with pinions poised, we shadow the sea with our sails and reelingly cleave the brine.

1— Animal as Folio

Melville combines the etymological and natural aspects of species (more like the predecessors of Buffon than Buffon himself, though B. is the referent given). Note the Chondropterygii (swordfish) and hangers-on in *Mardi*.

> One of them was right under the shark, nibbling at his ventral fin; another above, hovering about his dorsal appurtenance; one on each flank; and a frisking fifth pranking about his nose, seemingly having something to say of a confidential nature. They were of a bright, steel-blue color alternated with jet-black stripes, with glistening bellies of a silver white. Clinging to the back of the shark were four or five remoras, or sucking fish, snaky parasites impossible to remove from whatever they adhere to without detroying their lives. The remora has little power in swimming; hence its sole locomotion is on the backs of larger fish. Leech-like, it sticketh closer than a false brother in prosperity, closer than a beggar to the benevolent, closer than Webster to the Constitution. But it feeds upon what it clings to; its feelers having a direct communication with the esophagus.

In *Moby Dick*, the Pacific zoo has been bound as a single folio in the whale.

2— Totemism

Approximately the first third of *Mardi* is a consistent and suspenseful adventure, leading, eventually, to the capture of Yillah, who has both a white migrational history and a Polynesian legend-birth (Melville's two worlds). But after the narrator has her stolen from him, Melville abandons this story, and, in the guise of pursuing the quest for a lost maiden, converts it into a long etiological and mytho-historical debate. The islanders who accept the narrator as the god Taji are no ordinary archipeligans; they converse with him on matters of Plato, Dante, Spinoza, and Kant. They take a Pacific voyage outback of Western history, *through* Western history. The brilliant and charming conversation turns the previous *Mardi* into an erudite masque (by *Moby Dick* Melville has come to see that such a voyage is no tea party). Whereas Queequeg is a mute philosopher and a master of intuition and signs, Babbalanja is a Westerner. By Chapter 188 he is quoting Shakespeare's *Tempest* and Cicero's *Dream of Scipio*; he is giving Mardi's cosmology straight-on, like Ogotemmeli.[9] Though he is useless as a native, he is the perfect narrator for Melville's mestizo rebirth from totemic and Graeco-Christian sources.

> Then, as white flame from yellow, out from that starry cluster it emerged and brushed the astral crosses, crowns, and cups. And as in violet, tropic seas ships leave a radiant-white and firefly wake, so in long extension, tapering behind the vision, gleamed another Milky Way...
> We clove the air; passed systems, suns, and moons—what seem from Mardi's isles the glowworm stars.

That's powerful medicine for a native of the Pacific, and when Melville comes back to it ("Call me Ishmael. . ."), there's no doubt he will lay it far under, in the foundation of the book, leaving not a bare ripple on the surface dilemma of Western man. And so doing, he will prove that it's not just Babbalanja (articulate in his own language, for which Euro-American is ventriloquized)—that once aboard the same whaleship, we do come together as fate, we do have to swallow the same stuff, for our place, our equal place, on planet waters.

In *Typee* he is an American, secure in his geometry: a captive and runaway who is not responsible for the company he keeps (who keep him). *Mardi* is pure science fiction, with its lapses of real profundity into serial extravagance; the narrator is a forerunner of Heinlein's star-children. In *Moby Dick*, anthropologist and star-gazer come together. The narrative holds up because it is complete, like dream; irregular but complete. *Mardi* is the blueprint, and its flaws are the record we have of how Melville got to *Moby Dick*.

3— Philosophy

Mardi is too much a romance for Melville, in his darkness, to make it with, a little too dislocated in yearning to be back in the South Seas rescuing maidens and discoursing on creation with native philosophers: Melville's nostalgia, perhaps his regret at not using the time well. The book is filled with the filings of Melville's core: trauma, memory, eternity, nonhuman intelligence, hieroglyph, origin, biogenesis, stars. But they are set off as single flares, in the loose arena of the tale. *Moby Dick* comes after Herman has given up. He will never find it, but he will forever be the source of its recurrence. Its texture is as rough as wood, and it stands before *Mardi* as a glacier docs before a handmade diamond. *Moby Dick* is subtitled *The Whale*; *Mardi: And A Voyage Hither*. This is the whole difference. And there are moments in *Mardi* which are borrowed whole out of an unwritten *Moby Dick*:

> And like a frigate, I am full with a thousand souls; and as on, on, on I scud before the wind, many mariners rush up from the orlop below, like miners from caves, running across my decks; opposite braces are pulled; and this way and that, the great yards swing round on their axes; and boisterous speaking trumpets are heard, and contending orders to save the good ship from the shoals. Shoals, like nebulous vapors, shoring the white reef of the Milky Way, against which the wrecked worlds are dashed, strowing all the strand with their Himmaleh keels and ribs. . .
>
> In me, many worthies recline and converse. I list to St. Paul, who argues the doubts of Montaigne; Julian the Apostate cross-questions Augustine; and Thomas-a-Kempis unrolls his old black letters for all to

decipher. Zeno murmurs maxims beneath the hoarse shout of Democritus; and though Democritus laugh loud and long, and the sneer of Pyrrho be seen, yet divine Plato, and Proclus, and Verulam are of my counsel; and Zoroaster whispered me before I was born. I walk a world that is mine; and enter many nations, as Mungo Park rested in African cots; I am served like Bajazet—Bacchus my butler, Virgil my minstrel, Philip Sidney my page. My memory is a life beyond birth; my memory, my library of the Vatican, its alcoves all endless perspectives, eve-tinted by crosslights from Middle Age oriels.

C— Psychology (*Pierre* briefly)

Moby Dick convinced the author's family of his madness. Olson says they tried to ship him off to Europe. Oliver Wendell Holmes, the family physician, was called in, but by that time he had written *Pierre*, which is as much a turning inside-out of *Moby Dick* as Dorn's *Gunslinger* is of Olson's *Maximus*. According to Metcalf, contemporaries thought the author of *Pierre* should be confined to a mental institution, the sooner the better.

It is as if the tragedy and sorrow of *The Whale* were, in its completion, the breaking of the sybilline connection, the final loss of the Marquesan medium—a sadness so remote and ungauged that it becomes the individual destiny of Pierre, in another body, another birth.

The Whale, in the Jungian sense, is Melville's mythological journey to the underworld of prior events. Pierre goes back *himself*; he needs no ocean or cosmic journey; he is not an archetype or Odysseus; he is himself the philosopher, the "rebel without a cause," the crew of the *Pequod* joined as modern man. He transforms his social world, stretching it, as Melville does the Pacific. In a desperate attempt to claim the memory beyond birth, he engages in incest, poverty, bigamy, disinheritance, and general squalor. He is a forerunner of wealthy revolutionaries, political and sexual, who throw aside genealogy and taboo as mere symptom and plunge into world-shaping with their own lives as the clay. Pierre is a changer of consciousness; once he discovers he is bound by a curse (that will someday be called Oedipal), he scorns it and sacrifices himself to psychosis and martyrdom. In this he proves that the tragic hero can escape his literary fate by rejecting the traditionally glorious circumstances of his downfall, that Hamlet can flee Hamlet and still feel the sting. Like Ahab, he attacks the mask, blasphemously and without hope of success. *Pierre*, in a totally different way than *The Tempest*, enlarges upon *Hamlet*, but then it is *Moby Dick* that takes *The Tempest* into the Pacific.

Melville would also be a wild man before he would submit to a humane analysis of his demons and a dutiful exorcism. He did not have the present illusion of therapy and therapeutics, that we could be happy, fulfilled.

Meanwhile *Moby Dick* hadn't sold out the meager first printing, and wouldn't in his lifetime.

IV. THE WHALE HUNT

is the true cosmological journey of the nineteenth century universe.
is no longer available to us as such (hence the alienated reading of *Moby Dick* as an adventure story or a tale of nature:

> The Whale is not Hemingway's fish
> is not Faulkner's bear.

And if this event is to be translated into late twentieth century terms, we must discover its germ forms. For there is no kingdom that stands yet so big, which comes from an original historical unity. Our diminishment is exactly by our specialization.

A— The Bio-Topological

In the nineteenth century, biology was the main source of "creation news:" the living was the residue of the divine, and the hard landscape was a secondary stageset. Teratology, the study of monsters, was still a formidable science, entering, on one level, into the global census, and, on a deeper level, into the secrets of form. The whale was the proof of a mystery, a hidden shuttle; because the mystery was not known did not make it any less the proof.

Massiveness alone does not make the case in the nineteenth century, but in the whale, size was combined with the following in an irresistible equation:

1— Birth, regency, and death in the Great World Ocean; ability to dive in that ocean without conversion or insanity.

2— Intelligence and dignity.

3— The extreme smallness of other creatures, such as the spider or worm, who exist with no less integrity and with comparable intelligence, and, by their existence simultaneous with whales, stretch the biological order from the behemoth to the minute without distortion or malignancy. Size and shape are deformed within the continuous properties of the message.

> Unerringly impelling this dead, impregnable, uninjurable wall, and this most buoyant thing within; there swims behind it all a mass of tremendous life, only to be adequately estimated as piled wood is—by the cord; and all obedient to one volition, as the smallest insect.
> "The Battering-Ram."

115

By its sheer existence in the deep, the whale proved not only that vital plasma could heap itself massively in space but could, up to a point marked by the whale, transcend that heaping with subtle internal functions. Despite his size, the whale is a single consciousness, ruling a domain the way any sparrow or lion does.

The whale also marked the limits of Melville's cosmology: its breadth, its range into the far Pacific, its Biblical etymology, its sacred reappearance in Marquesan theology. What the natives were in *Typee*, the whale (not Queequeg) is in *Moby Dick*. It allows, in fact requires, the brutal paganism of the non-Western world one way and the Christian brutality of the Western politicians and whale-hunters coming back the other.

Our only suitable equivalent to the bio-topological whale of Melville's time is the star, the star of science fiction, astrophysics, and aerospace. As the master of his own archaeology, Melville managed to keep whale and star in their accurate relative positions, so that, at key points, they merge, as if in prefigurement of the new century, but, as always, in recovery of an older coherence.

> Nor when expandingly lifted by your subject, can you fail to trace out great whales in the starry heavens, and boats in pursuit of them; as when long filled with thoughts of war the Eastern nations saw armies locked in battle among the clouds. Thus at the North have I chased Leviathan round and round the Pole with the revolutions of the bright points that first defined him to me. And beneath the effulgent Antarctic skies I have boarded the Argo-Navis, and joined the chase against the starry Cetus far beyond the utmost stretch of Hydrus and the Flying Fish.
> "Of Whales in Paint."

Whales are stars, certainly for the same original reason that Poseidon is the sea. One reader of *Moby Dick* said that the first time the book really struck home to him was when he realized that Ishmael was seeing constellations above the ocean that never appeared in Northern Hemisphere skies. Cetus itself lies just at the horizon between Northern and Southern skies; thus the whaling ship can sight its way by following the different neighbors Cetus finds itself among. The same bright points suggest the beginning of civilization (as in *Hamlet's Mill*), and the remoteness and outwardness of the entire vision. It is a curious irony that the Brazilian constellation "the Jaguar," lying beneath a fisherman with a net and a swarm of wasps, is the European constellation "Cetus, the Whale," lying beneath Orion, the Hunter, and the Pleiades.[10]

As our search for original form has moved beyond the purely biological into questions of matter and galactic generation, we have broken our agreement with the animal kingdom: the whale, as reigning king, is victim. The genetic is now inextricably buried in the morphological, first in the current use of Darwin's laws to trace the origin of the living back to the non-living (star, carbon, and stone), and second in the crystalline and electromagnetic complexities of that new universal chemistry. Melville is early stumbling this way.

> Even Scoresby, the justly renowned Right Whaleman, after giving us a stiff full length of the Greenland Whale, and three or four delicate miniatures of narwhales and porpoises, treats us to a series of classical engravings of boat hooks, chopping knives, and grapnels; and with the microscopic diligence of a Leuwenhoeck submits to the inspection of a shivering world ninety-six facsimilies of magnified Arctic snow crystals.
> "Of the Less Erroneous Pictures of Whales, and the True Pictures
> of Whaling Scenes."

Simultaneous investigations of primary elements and the physical make-up of heavenly bodies have come to marry living and non-living entities to the same chemistry, compromising the whale's unique status and its previously unmatched union of composition and size. As chemistry becomes universal rather than vital, the whale merges with a new class of objects. Though it remains large and unusual in the phyla of the Earth, it is no longer spectacular in a cosmic framework. It is just another animal, neither chemically nor atomically unique.

· But it is just as much a mistake to think the whale has lost its crown only because the stars are larger as to assume that its size alone entitled it to the crown originally. The scope of the heavens has been known before, if not as profoundly. It is because stars are essentially similar to whales that whales are no longer needed to mark the outer limits of morphological complexity. Once, the stars were made of ethereal matter, utterly removed from terrestrial biology; later they were real but inert, separated from our world by the vacuum of space. Now the universe is a single elemental pool; the vacuum is filled by energies, radiations, particles, and gravities. The hydrogen and iron in suns and planets *is* the hydrogen and iron in plants and animals, and in mind.

The ladders and hierarchies of the nineteenth century taxonomist, who presided over the whale's unofficial coronation, stand as trivial before the overall taxonomy of electrons, cells, polarities, and intelligence. The universe is created, either Big Bang or Steady State, and, from there, matter flows from the original fires into living systems, in a process so intricate and serpentine as the defy imagination. It is no longer acceptable to consider star-suns dead furnaces; they are more like life-windmills, drawing from pools at their centers, blowing to the ends of creation. In some systems, not terribly remote from science any longer, the stars are living beings, perceiving, as we do, the space in which they are contained. Note Rodney Collin's network of intelligent suns, or certain parapsychological re-evaluations of sentience, memory, and aura.

One may reject the more mystical romance, but they will have a hard time returning stars and whales to their respective nineteenth century statuses. Stars are more complex, more active, and more ambiguous than ever. They rival living systems in their condensation and discontinuous shapes. Quasars, for instance, operate at inexplicable ratios of intensity and size, and seem totally out of the scale and landscape of the known universe. They are the derelicts and buoy-warnings of some other internalized space. Pulsars have awesome density and gravitation; they are not as big as stars, but their suck in place is so great they threaten to turn space inside-out. Their pulse is more accurate than a cesium clock. Before beauties like these, the whale, dragging his hunters along with him, returns, somewhat sadly and with other endangered species, to the disrupted garden of terrestrial life (despite the very real wonders the nineteenth century naturalist saw). The same intelligence which has brought the deep cosmological terrors of the stars into worldly ken has developed instruments for destroying and eliminating whales. If whale (then) is star (now)—it is not at the expense of whaleness, but in terms of Melville's precise log, following the transits that lie between his time and ours. If we think Melville fails as an astronomer, then we might also think it is "the poor threatened whale pursued by pathological man." But the whale remains, long past extinction, where we cannot escape him. Weak and erring man has not only contrived the tools of whale obliteration but forged the instruments and telescopes of this cosmology without moving one iota out of *Moby Dick*. It's that clear and heavy a sky.

[From another angle, we might say: it is not so much that science has discovered the implicit intelligence and intricacy of stars as that it has severely reduced its assessment of such qualities in living and intelligent beings. Ethology, social science, and behavioral psychology have consigned many of the previously-acknowledged "free movements" of animals (and people) to a more compelled system. So stars are no more inanimate or unwilled than we. The so-called "causes" of evolution, in the stars, are hierarchically the remote causes of individual acts of consciousness, as well as of general consciousness. It does not require traditional astrology to have man's volition co-opted by stars.]

Additionally, the exobiological application of Darwinian law to planets larger than Earth (Saturn and Jupiter, in particular, within our own system) fills a tentative cosmic taxonomy with beasts many times the size of the whale.

> It did not resemble a tree at all but a jellyfish—a medusa, such as might be met trailing its tentacles as it drifted along the warm eddies of the Gulf Stream.

This medusa was two kilometers across and its scores of dangling tentacles were hundreds of meters long. They swayed slowly back and forth in perfect unison, taking more than a minute for each complete undulation—almost as if the creature were clumsily rowing itself through the sky...

...High intelligence could only develop among predators—not among the drifting browsers of either sea or air. The mantas were far closer to him than was this monstrous bag of gas; and anyway, who could *really* sympathize with a creature a hundred thousand time larger than a whale?   Arthur Clarke: "A Meeting with Medusa."

Melville's precision far outweighs any context lost by the shift. His descriptions are chillingly local; if we would no longer look where *he* did, he is already where we are looking. Compare the following, from *Moby Dick*, to the above, quasi-Jovian; you see it will be a long time before we take a space odyssey larger than Melville's.

A vast pulpy mass, furlongs in length and breadth, of a glancing cream-color, lay floating on the water, innumerable long arms radiating from its centre, and curling and twisting like a nest of anacondas, as if blindly to clutch at any hapless object within reach. No perceptible face or front did it have; no conceivable token of either sensation or instinct; but undulated there on the billows an unearthly, formless, chance-like apparition of life.   "Squid."

Which is outer space? Who has the fuller sense of an intrustion?

Melville's topology of the Pacific and the whale compares more closely to Kip Thorne's description of gravitational collapse. i.e., what happens when a star sucks in all its material and disappears from the perceptible universe. The twisting of space required for such an event is the absolute horizon for the raw universe (by Thorne's system). The condition of singularity that follows is, perhaps, one of ultimate repose, but the explosion that precedes it is astronomically pathological, at least in the sense that a star must destroy itself to recover its innermost events. And this is a pathology we would associate with both Melville and Ahab. If the black hole is Ahab, the White Whale is light; the black hole is necessary because the gradual deterioration of matter brings about an imbalance of energy, needing fresh matter (via rays or quanta) to keep reality going.

Is it that by its indefiniteness it shadows forth the heartless voids and immensities of the universe, and thus stabs us from behind with the thought of annihilation, when beholding the white depths of the milky way? ...and when we proceed further, and consider that the mystical cosmetic which produces every one of her hues, the great principle of life, for ever remains white or colorless in itself, and if operating without medium upon matter, would touch all objects, even tulips and roses, with its own blank tinge—pondering all this, the palsied universe lies before us a leper; and like wilful travellers in Lapland, who refuse to wear colored and coloring glasses upon their eyes, so the wretched infidel gazes himself blind at the monumental white shroud that wraps all the prospect around him. And of all these things the Albino Whale was the symbol. Wonder ye then at the fiery hunt?   "The Whiteness of the Whale."

But if the source can be fire and light, it can also be a sacred text, either a more ancient *Bible* or the qabbalistic plan from which creation comes because divination precedes matter. The whale is enclosed in an archetype of a whale, which is a star also. At the same time it reduces his range, it increases it by tying him to his original undiminished form. In moments of intense astronomy, Melville does not forget his history (as Thorne does); he does not abandon planetary chronicles in an obsession with creationary horizon. So whaling has a mythopoetic moment in which it is indispensible to planet-formation.

When Brahma, or the God of Gods, saith the Shaster, resolved to recreate the world after one of its periodical dissolutions, he gave birth to Vishnoo, to preside over the work; but the Vedas, or mystical books, whose perusal would seem to have been indispensable to Vishnoo before beginning the creation, and which therefor must have contained something in the shape of practical hints to young architects, these Vedas were lying at the bottom of the waters; so Vishnoo became incarnate in a whale, and sounding down in him to the uttermost depths, rescued the sacred volumes. Was not this Vishnoo a whaleman, then? even as a man who rides a horse is called a hoseman?
                                        "The Honor and Glory of Whaling."

The chinks and crannies Melville intuits may be Newtonian in architecture, but the overall thrust of *Moby Dick* is cosmic and astrophysical. Melville may have sat up with shipmates on long nights debating free will versus predestination, but he is less concerned with the abstract metaphysics of morality than the brilliance of the immediate world. He deals a powerful atomism, and the universal is stuffed into its discrete quanta of event.

Yes, these eyes are windows, and this body of mine is the house. What a pity they didn't stop up the chinks and the crannies though, and thrust in a little lint here and there. But it's too late to make any improvements now. The universe is finished; the copestone is on, and the chips were carted off a million years ago.   "The Carpet-bag."

If the universe is finished, it is cosmology which is not. The moment of creation may be over in terms of law, but not in terms of perception, which is our bias. The lint is what philosophy strains against, to make itself as legitimate as reality. A million years is Melville's radio noise, dilated with time: those events of a previous epoch which totally define this one yet no longer occur (thus are not part of the actual story). Compare Dorn:

> ... the road had a way of increasing while its length was at any point known, like the universe with each new refinement of the instruments possesses a 'new' largeness and is brighter than before expected.
>
> "Of Eastern Newfoundland."

> We are of the end of the leeching which produced us. A spoonful left at the bottom, very refined, pure stuff, the final dry powder, the dust that lives. The crack it will go into, the crack in the real. The quality is obvious to everyone though of course like quality it can be faked as some revival called a revolution. It isn't automatic by living that you get your own song.   "Some Business Recently Transacted in the White World."

Moby Dick stands to Melville as the universe does either to its creator or its cosmologist. Cash is as germinal, then, as fire and cosmic dust.

> But I now leave my Cetological System standing thus unfinished, even as the great Cathedral of Cologne was left, with the crane still standing upon the top of the uncompleted tower. For small erections may be finished by their first architects; grand ones, true ones, ever leave the copestone to posterity. God keep me from ever completing anything. This whole book is but a draught—nay, but the draught of a draught! Oh, Time, Strength, Cash and Patience!"   "Cetology"

In Thorne's cosmology, everything is very mechanical. The hole is made necessary by a tinker toy geometry. The light, the last visible photon, is the means by which pulsar or whale is known at all, behind which lies confusion, pathology, or malevolence. Melville operates without instruments, so his cosmology is: *the same thing is there if you know it is there.* Thorne's credo is: *something must be there.* Though delicate and sensitive, with structural resemblances to Melville, it is basically schematic, and its inventor runs the risk of falling out of the crow's nest for dozing while at sea.

> There is one way in which the matter might escape being crushed. There might be a topological hole inside the photon 3-surface through which the matter of the star could flow without being crushed to zero volume. The matter might then emerge, bubbling upward like a spring in the mountains, in some other region of our own universe or in some other universe.   Kip S. Thorne: "Gravitational Collapse," *Scientific American*,
> November, 1967.

In *Moby Dick*, a collapse is also the topological resolution, and a natural distortion rolls over the event horizon leaving a single herald to mark the spot.

...and so the bird of heaven, with archangelic shrieks, and his imperial beak thrust upwards, and his whole captive form folded in the flag of Ahab, went down with his ship, which, like Satan, would not sink to hell till she had dragged a living part of heaven along with her, and helmeted herself with it.

Now small fowls flew screaming over the yet yawning gulf; a sullen white surf beat against its steep sides; then all collapsed, and the great shroud of the sea rolled on as it rolled five thousand years ago.

"The Chase—Third Day."

Melville has no wish to balance the energies in the universe, either thermodynamically or spiritually. He chooses moments of momentary balance or uncanny assignation. Olson attributes to Melville an intuition of inertial presence, that between remote and exiled positions there lies a torque. This is the condition of his astrophysics, not objective observation and measurement, but a profound awareness of the bubbling, the concentration, the fluidity of form, the lotus itself.

I say so strange a dreaminess did there then reign all over the ship and all over the sea, only broken by the intermitting dull sound of the sword, that it seemed as if this were the Loom of Time, and I myself were a shuttle mechanically weaving and weaving away at the Fates.

"The Mat-Maker."

The air around suddenly vibrated and tingled, as it were, like the air over intensely heated plates of iron. Beneath this atmospheric waving and curling, and partially beneath a thin layer of water, also, the whales were swimming.   "The First Lowering."

So there is no earthly way of finding out precisely what the whale really looks like. And the only mode in which you can derive even a tolerable idea of his living contour, is by going a whaling yourself; but by so doing, you run no small risk of being eternally stove and sunk by him."

"Of the Monstrous Pictures of Whales."

An early chortle over Newtonian physics.

For, when the line is darting out, to be seated then in the boat, is like being seated in the midst of the manifold whizzings of a steam-engine in full play, when every flying beam, and shaft, and wheel, is grazing you. It is worse; for you cannot sit motionless in the heart of these perils, because the boat is rocking like a cradle, and you are pitched one way and the other, without the slightest warning; and only by a certain self-adjusting buoyancy and simultaneousness of volition and action, can you escape being made a Mazeppa of, and run away with where the all-seeing sun himself could never pierce you out.   "The Line.

The red tide now poured from all sides of the monster like brooks down a hill. His tormented body rolled not in brine but in blood, which bubbled and seethed for furlongs behind in their wake. The slanting sun playing upon this crimson pond in the sea, sent back its reflection into every face, so that they all glowed to each other like red men. And all the while, jet after jet of white smoke was agonizingly shot from the spiracle of the whale, and vehement puff after puff from the mouth of the excited headsman; as at every dart, hauling in upon his crooked lance (by the line attached to it), Stubb straightened it again and again, by a few rapid blows against the gunwale, then again and again sent it into the whale.
"Stubb Kills a Whale."

The vast white headless phantom floats further and further from the ship, and every rod that it so floats, what seem square roods of sharks and cubic roods of fowls, augment the murderous din.   "The Funeral."

...the Sperm Whale's head embraces nearly one third of his entire bulk, and completely to suspend such a burden as that, even by the immense tackles of a whaler, this were as vain a thing as to attempt weighing a Dutch barn in jewellers' scales.   "The Sphynx."

Silence reigned over the before tumultuous but now deserted deck. An intense copper calm, like a universal yellow lotus, was more and more unfolding its noiseless measureless leaves upon the sea.   "The Sphynx."

Howard Vincent tells me this is the one image in the book whose source eludes him. If this is true, and he is that thorough, then the lotus sits at the dead center of *Moby Dick*, where space and mind and inertia begin, guarding Melville's archetypal source. From this singularity the rest of *Moby Dick* like a light show springs. True or not (and who could say for sure?), it is a perfect mandala for the book.

And they stuck to it till they did gain it; when instantly, a swift tremor was felt running like lightning along the keel, as the strained line, scraping beneath the ship, suddenly rose to view under her bows, snapping and quivering; and so flinging off its drippings, that the drops fell like bits of broken glass on the water, while the whale beyond also rose to sight, and once more the boats were free to fly.
"Stubb and Flask Kill a Right Whale; and Then Have a Talk Over Him."

"But as if this vast local power in the tendinous tail were not enough, the whole bulk of the Leviathan is knit over with a warp and woof of muscular fibres and filaments, which passing on either side the loins and running down into the flukes, insensibly blend with them, and largely contribute to their might; so that in the tail the confluent measureless force of the whole whale seems concentrated to a point. Could annihilation occur to matter, this were the thing to do it.   "The Tail."

This "confluent measureless force" of the whale must be the inertial equivalent of the "noiseless unfolding lotus;" related as well to the malignity and sentience behind the mask, but deeper to the drum. Plus its precognition of Thorne's collapsing star, itself a literary brother to the sinking *Pequod*. All these suggestions float about the same tenuous center: the profound noiselessness, the sphynx, the shedding of something, of radiation, of leaves, the concentration along the flukes, the annihilation of matter. "The absolute condition of present things," Herman tells us. There is an eternal object both intermittent and motionless in back of the narrative of *Moby Dick*, reminding us of the river with which Olson ends *Maximus VI* ("nothing all the way/of the hollow of the Diorite/from glacial time to this soft summer night/with the river in this respite solely/an interruption of itself"). It sits in the lastingness of the present, with the insistence of a glacier or a sun. The journey of the *Pequod* is engraved on its bulk but in minute Palaeolithic script. It is the end. And long after the story is finished, it still sits.

> Yes, the long calm was departing. A low advancing hum was soon heard; and then like to the tumultuous masses of block-ice when the great river Hudson breaks up in Spring, the entire host of whales came tumbling upon their inner centre, as if to pile themselves up in one common mountain.   "The Grand Armada."

The inertial passages suggest the physics of Melville's work, his delicate response to subtleties of mass, energy, and gravity. The pure star-whale comparisons are more like astrology, or astrophysics. The whale moves like a star and is subject to the same forces that create and destroy stars, even as stars are subject to galactic rhythms. All creatures, astrophysically, are joined in a network of response and obedience to the overall charm or eros that pervades the universe and makes of it a zodiac. The whale painted on an ancient sky fragment, with angels at its quadrants, is an accurate sounding of the whale at sea.

> Besides, when making a passage from one feeding-ground to another, the Sperm Whales, guided by some infallible instinct—say, rather, secret intelligence from the Deity—along a given ocean-line with such undeviating exactitude, that no ship ever sailed her course, by any chart, with one tithe of such marvelous precision. Though, in these cases, the direction taken by any one whale be straight as a surveyor's parallel, and though the line of advance be strictly confined to its own unavoidable, straight wake, yet the arbitrary *vein* in which at these times he is said to swim, generally embraces some few miles in width (more or less, as the vein is presumed to expand or contract); but never exceeds the visual sweep from the whale-ship's mast-heads, when circumspectly gliding along this magic zone. The sum is, that at particular seasons within the

breadth and along that path, migrating whales may with great confidence be looked for.   "The Chart."

And then the meteorology of whales, weighing them as clouds, right down to their buoyancy and magnetic charge.

> Like a savage tigress that tossing in the jungle overlays her own cubs, so the sea dashes even the mightiest whales against the rocks, and leaves them there side by side with the split wrecks of ships.   "Brit."

Or Melville makes of his whale a clock, on which he measures all other clocks and calendars, plus biorhythms, georhythms, geysers, bird migrations, and then: this is Herman, once again checking in on us, in our futuristic time, from the actual moment of the writing of the book.

> That for six thousand years—and no one knows how many millions of ages before—the great whales should have been spouting all over the sea, and sprinkling and mistifying the gardens of the deep, as with so many sprinkling or mistifying pots; and that for some centuries back, thousands of hunters should have been close by the fountain of the whale, watching these sprinklings and spoutings—that all this should be, and yet, that down to this blessed minute (fifteen and a quarter minutes past one o'clock P.M. of this sixteenth day of December, A.D., 1851), it should still remain a problem, whether these spoutings are, after all, really water, or nothing but vapor—this is surely a noteworthy thing.   "The Fountain."

As Ahab approaches the whale, his journey becomes more and more cosmological. He grasps at the Egyptian beginnings of things, the gods the gods of Hesiod are taken from, originally the stars, imposing on the Earth its calendars and migrations of peoples, as the movements of whales impose the "seasons" of the whale-boats through their own "zodiac." Melville preserved, no doubt unintentionally, a heritage which Hesiod marks only on our blind side of the great Atlantean and Hittite divide.

> And where Ahab's chances of accomplishing his object have hitherto been spoken of, allusion has only been made to whatever wayside, antecedent, extra prospects where his, ere a particular set time or place were attained, when all possibilities would become probabilities, and, as Ahab fondly thought, every possibility the next thing to a certainty. That particular set time and place were conjoined in the one technical phrase—the Season-on-the-Line. For there and then, for several consecutive years, Moby Dick had been periodically descried, lingering in those waters for awhile, as the sun, in its annual round, loiters for a predicted interval in any one sign of the Zodiac.   "The Chart.'

Melville finally brought pyramid and mast together, movement of Earth through buoyancy of the heavens as movement of ship upon planetary waters. As stars come into view over the horizon, so do whales from below. The imperciptible motion of the Earth into new cosmology becomes perceptible when the astronomer is priest, mounts the pyramid, and sights the changing of an order.

> And that the Eyptians were a nation of mast-head standers is an assertion based upon the general belief among archaeologists, that the first pyramids were founded for astronomical purposes: a theory singularly supported by the peculiar stair-like formation of all four sides of these edifices; whereby, with prodigious long upliftings of their legs, those old astronomers were wont to mount to the apex, and sing out new stars; even as the look-outs of a modern ship sing out for a sail, or a whale just bearing in sight.   "The Mast-head."

B— The Psychoanalytic

1— The Original Theme

Moby Dick is not, in the usual sense, a psychological novel; Melville does not explore motivation with the precision of a Dostoevski. Emotions and thoughts are taken as ripples in the cosmic shape; they emerge distantly from the hierarchies their completions again give rise to (in a cycle that ties even the most trivial melodramas to planet history). Melville diagnoses the profound and enduring fact of trauma in nature, the final depths of what can no longer be felt but upon which creatures act (whales as inevitably as men). A once-inflicted pain, or the code of an ancient message, is retained in the plasma of the universe, indelibly; it becomes a repetitive obsessive activity, detached from its source. The stab is a seed, and its branches entwine with the branches of the body, encompass the nervous system, and are passed on in the blood. Melville knew this quite apart from any mythology of curses or genealogical doom; it was science, not haunting, and that is why he is an early depth psychologist.

Unless transformed by a powerful healing event, the traumatic moment itself is fatal. The wound becomes a scar, and while the outer mark alone is visible, seemingly moribund, the shock lingers and seeks to establish, if not its revenge, then its "economic" function in the psyche (to borrow, anachronistically, from Reich).

> Threading its way out from among his grey hairs, and continuing right down one side of his tawny scorched face and neck, till it disappeared in his clothing, you saw a slender rod-like mark, lividly whitish. It resembled that perpendicular seam sometimes made in the straight, lofty trunk of a great tree, when the upper lightning tearingly darts down it, and without wrenching a single twig, peels and grooves out the bark from top to bottom, ere running off into the soil, leaving the tree still greenly alive, but branded.   "Ahab."

All sentient beings are so marked, as a consequence and condition of their sentience. Individuals die, but the events linger, in the species and the planet. Even if we were to start over again, with babes, there would be the difficulties of birth and death, and the combined mercilessness of astronomical cycles, territoriality, and instinct.

> As strange misgrown masses gather in the knot-holes of the noblest oaks when prostrate, so from the points which the whale's eyes had once occupied, now protruded blind bulbs, horribly pitiable to see. But pity there was none. For all his old age, and his one arm, and his blind eyes, he must die the death and be murdered, in order to light the gay bridals and other merry-makings of men, and also to illuminate the solemn churches that preach unconditional inoffensiveness by all to all.
>
> "The Pequod Meets the Virgin."

Before Freud, there was no formal map of the unconscious mind. Though Freud sketched but an intuitive tracery of nervous processes, it has served since, even more prominently than physiologies of the brain (which would be, at best, literal latter-day phrenologies). Melville's forms suggest Freud's as Galileo's maps of the Moon remain the rough condition of our Moon geographies. Mind, perception, and philosophy are muddied with external objects in a pool that proves our existence as well as the simultaneity of all other things. Melville had both the advantage and disadvantage of not knowing about cathexis, libido, memory loss, and so on. He read the nervous system directly, from the winged and tattooed messengers.

The whale is a creature of feeling. It bears its young in human fashion. It has organs of great sensuality and refinement, enclosed in a numbing bulk (similar to the armor and lesions in which men enclose their poignancies). Through the cruel and provocative deeds of their fellow mammals, whales suffer incredible anxiety, indignity, and mutilation. Men must stand before this, as before their own kind, insensate of the damage they cause because they are also numb. The whale is a giant and exposed humanoid, and though *Moby Dick* goes to sea after the oil in its body, with the men of the *Pequod*, it never abandons this perspective.

> For, suspended in those watery vaults, floated the forms of the nursing mothers of the whales, and those that by their enormous girth seemed shortly to become mothers. The lake, as I have hinted, was to a considerable depth exceedingly transparent; and as human infants while suckling will calmly and fixedly gaze away from the breast, as if leading two different lives at the same time; and while yet drawing mortal nourishment, be still spiritually feasting upon some unearthly reminiscence; —even so did the young of these whales seem looking up towards us, but not at us, as if we were but a bit of gulf-weed in their new-born sight. Floating on their sides, the mothers also seemed quietly eyeing us. One of

these little infants, that from certain queer tokens seemed hardly a day old, might have measured some fourteen feet in length, and some six feet in girth. He was a little frisky; though as yet his body seemed scarce yet recovered from that irksome position it had so lately occupied in the maternal reticule; where, tail to head, and all ready for the final spring, the unborn whale lies bent like a Tartar's bow. The delicate side-fins, and the palms of his flukes, still freshly retained the plaited crumpled appearance of a baby's ears newly arrived from foreign parts.

"The Grand Armada."

Where it is not feeling and sentience, it is some equally compelling handwriting.

The magnetic energy, as developed in the mariner's needle, is, as all know, essentially one with the electricity beheld in heaven; hence it is not to be much marvelled at, that such things should be. In instances where the lightning has actually struck the vessel, so as to smite down some of the spars and rigging, the effect upon the needle has at times been still more fatal; all its loadstone virtue being annihilated, so that the before magnetic steel was of no more use than an old wife's knitting needle. But in either case, the needle never again, of itself, recovers the original virtue thus marred or lost; and if the binnacle compasses be affected, the same fate reaches all the others that may be in the ship; even were the lowermost one inserted into the kelson.   "The Needle."

And in the same universe, the same shipful of men is drawn irrevocably to a meeting with Moby Dick off the "cellular memory" in Ahab of the searing of his leg.

It is not improbable that this monomania in him took its instant rise *at the precise time* of his bodily dismemberment.

"Moby Dick.   (emphasis mine).

Which is recalled in the opening of "The Hat."

And now that at the proper time and place, after so long and wide a preliminary cruise, Ahab—all other whaling waters swept—seemed to have chased his foe into an ocean-fold, to slay him the more securely there; now, that he found himself hard by the very latitude and longitude where his tormenting wound had been inflicted; now that a vessel had spoken which on the very day preceding had actually encountered Moby Dick; —and now that all his successive meetings with various ships contrastingly concurred to show the demoniac indifference with which the White Whale tore his hunters, whether sinning or sinned against; now it was that there lurked a something in the old man's eyes, which it was hardly sufferable for feeble souls to see.

Starbuck approaches Ahab and pleads with him to turn back from Moby Dick. He softens him with images of children, families, meadows, sun (we recall his equally unsuccessful attempt to keep Flask from stabbing the dying whale, how whales are "people" too, and want to be left in peace, to nurse and play with their children, and find each other lovingly in the deep). This should be enough, in the humane order, to turn Ahab back, but Ahab has pased into the cosmic order, and his transit has the certainty of a planet or Egyptian parchment. The scar precedes the severing of the leg; the trauma precedes the scar and is preceded in the karmic order by some earlier form yet. The moment is almost Tibetan: Ahab completes a dark event and brings to an end a cycle, a world-age (in Melville himself, the dark inter-regnum of *Pierre* follows). Just as Ahab never brought that ship home, and the men to see their families, so Herman never brought the ship home either (with his children), never made it back from Fayaway and the Pacific shaman (the tale Metcalf tells in *Genoa*).

> What is it, what nameless, inscrutable, unearthly thing is it, what cozening, hidden lord and master, and cruel remorseless emperor commands me; that against all natural lovings and longings, I so keep pushing, and crowding, and jamming myself on all the time; recklessly making me ready to do what in my own proper, natural heart, I durst not so much as dare? Is Ahab, Ahab? Is it I, God, or who that lifts this arm? But if the great sun move not of himself; but is as an errand-boy in heaven; nor one single star can revolve, but by some invisible power; how then can this one small heart beat; this one small brain think thoughts; unless God does that beating, does that thinking, does that living, and not I. By heaven, man, we are turned round and round in this world, like yonder windlass, and Fate is the handspike. And all the time, lo! that smiling sky, and this unsounded sea! Look! see yon Albicore! who put it into him to chase and fang that flying fish? Where do murderers go, man! Who's to doom, when the judge himself is dragged to the bar?
>
> "The Symphony."

So Hamlet stands under a new mill. But the problem is the same. How can we act, when actions defy each other? Why were we sold consciousness, a useless trinket, under such duress? What power does the judge have when he is also judged?; the mind when it is also minded? These questions ring out through modern literature, linguistic theory, and psychoanalysis; but they are still Hamlet—same depot, another, another mill. Melville found them exactly where Freud, excavating neurosis, came upon the ruins of Egypt, at the turning of the centuries. And now we inherit *Moby Dick* as naturally as they could not. For this is exactly where we are, and Ahab is our chosen captain. The whole environmental argument (say, against nuclear power plants) is Starbuck's, down under the psychology of it.

2— Secondary Marks

Trauma and scar is only one of the forms in which the "eternal mark" appears in *Moby Dick*. The Egyptian and Mississippian petroglyphs are as accurate clues to mind and will as the existential ponderings of a troubled character, despite the fact they no longer "think" or "feel." Any distortion, even a surficial striation, is the manifestation of an inward germ. There is no cure but there is also no source. There is only a morphologist's reconstruction of the intricacy (the scar on Ahab, the lightning mark on the oak, the birth-tattoos on the tortoise's shell). These marks document our present location in demonic space. They appear as conditions do, within conditions, and are not separable or interpretable in the modus in which they occur. Hence, when Melville cites a clue, he is as attracted by its remoteness and obscurity as by the clarity of its being there. Revelation, where it is brightest, is also occultation. The clue, classically, deepens the mystery.

I would distinguish three related categories of marks in *Moby Dick*:

NATURE	ART	PSYCHE
Eolith	Hieroglyph	Wound
Animal Trail	Tattoo	Scar
Birthmark	Petroglyph	Trauma
Hieroglyph		

Of course, archaeology and psychology overlap, and the marks made by man, even as they are conscious script for a moment, enter immediately into a hieroglyphic text. Economic and theological records, as the Mayan glyphs, end up in as unconscious a context as fossil lampshells. Arguments about whether particular designs were left by astronauts from other planets, Europeans travelling in the New World before the birth of Christ, or native scribes are irrelevant to the moment of a mark in nature. Even should the historical questions be satisfactorily resolved, the uncertain properties of language and translation would consign the event to other shadows. It is unclear how any of *our* messages will be read by gods or archaeologists.

The tattoo is the prototypical mark for this level of *Moby Dick*. Melville's involvement with body markings comes, at least in part, from his own narrow escape with being tattooed while a captive in the Pacific. The tattooing would have marked him for life as one outside Western culture, and it would also have bound him to a lineage of Marquesan ceremonialism (for, even though the tattoo is essentially an external mark, it is permanent as a decay that works from there *into* the flesh, even as the genetic works from its codons out *onto* the flesh). Just as nature is continuously inscribed in sourceless dictation, so men imprint their cosmology on themselves and their artifacts. And Queequeg copies his tattoes onto his coffin, suggesting, at once, the Egyptian and the Marquesan. He is as faithful to his gods as the naturalist whose dying act is the recording of a new species of beetle.

> Many spare hours he spent, in carving the lid with all manner of grotesque figures and drawings; and it seemed that hereby he was striving, in his rude way, to copy parts of the twisted tattooing on his body. And this tattooing had been the work of a departed prophet and seer of his island, who, by those hieroglyphic marks, had written out on his body a complete theory of the heavens and the earth, and a mystical treatise on the art of attaining truth; so that Queequeg in his own proper person was a riddle to unfold; a wondrous work in one volume; but whose mysteries not even himself could read, though his own live heart beat against them; and these mysteries were therefore destined in the end to moulder away with the living parchment whereon they were inscribed, and so be unsolved to the last. "Queequeg in his Coffin,"

If Melville were a self-conscious modernist, or an occultist (like Poe), he might have cast an ominous and ghostly coffin. Queequeg's automatic rendering of an ancient code from one impermanent parchment onto another in which the one shall be placed is a primary event in human consciousness. In the many-thousandth year of his own culture, the code is at least partially obsolete; it needs no ethereal refinement. Here messenger RNA lays its body onto the previously-sentenced strands, here the words are set in new triplets, here the actual material disappears. Caterpillar to moth. Tadpole to frog. The flow is continuous and visible, but the links are broken off into some other plane.

For Melville, there is one universal science and one philosophy; its branches include: archaeology, geology, astronomy, physiology, ethnography, and psychology. *Moby Dick* is the textbook of these working together in one reference, without acknowledgement of a prior or later separation.

> These mystic creatures, suddenly translated by night from unutterable solitudes to our peopled deck, affected me in a manner not easy to unfold. They seemed newly crawled forth from beneath the foundations of the world. Yea, they seemd the identical tortoises whereon the Hindoo plants this total sphere. . .
>
> As, lantern in hand, I scraped among the moss and behind the ancient scars of bruises received in many a sullen fall among the marly mountains of the isle—scars strangely widened, swollen, half obliterate, and yet distorted like those sometimes found in the bark of very hoary trees, I seemed an antiquary of a geologist, studying the bird-tracks and ciphers upon the exhumed slates trod by incredible creatures whose very ghosts are now defunct. *The Encantadas or Enchanted Isles.*

Melville's visit to the Galapagos Islands (from the account of which the above is taken) recalls the famous Darwinian journey to the same shrine.

Then, in describing the depths of Ahab, Melville mentions a place:

> ...where far beneath the fantastic towers of man's upper earth, his root of grandeur, his whole awful essence sits in bearded state; an antique buried beneath antiquities, and throned on torsoes!   "Moby Dick."

Likewise Fedallah:

> He was such a creature as civilized, domestic people in the temperate zone only see in their dreams, and that but dimly; but the like of whom now and then glide among the unchanging Asiatic communities, especially the Oriental isles to the east of the continent—those insulated, immemorial, unalterable countries, which even in these modern days still preserve much of the ghostly aboriginalness of earth's primal generations, when the memory of the first man was a distinct recollection, and all men his descendants, unknowing whence he came, eyed each other as real phantoms, and asked of the sun and the moon why they were created and to what end...'   "Ahab's Boat and Crew. Fedallah."

Melville has seen enough of humanity and the vast splintered migrations to realize that Biblical tradition, with its Mu and Mormon advocates (nascent in his time), is a dime-store account of the world's lineages. The whale likewise: not only his genetics and phylogeny, but the archetypal evolution behind such a beast, as the spirit descends into matter:

> Now, by all odds, the most ancient extant portrait anyways purporting to be the whale's, is to be found in the famous cavern-pagoda of Elephanta, in India. The Brahmins maintain that in the almost endless sculptures of that immemorial pagoda, all the trades and pursuits, every conceivable avocation of man, were prefigured ages before any of them actually came into being...   "Of the Monstrous Pictures of Whales."

From the theosophical to the historical-hermetic:

> Then, there are the Prodromus whales of old Scotch Sibbald, and Jonah's whale, as depicted in the prints of old Bibles and the cuts of old primers. What shall be said of these? As for the book-binder's whale winding like a vine-stalk round the stock of a descending anchor—as stamped and gilded on the backs and title-pages of many books both old and new—that is a very picturesque but purely fabulous creature, imitated, I take it, from the like figures on antique vases.
> "Of the Monstrous Pictures of Whales."

And then the genealogical, prefiguring the Galapagos tortoise:

> Was it not so, O Don Miquel! thou Chilian whale, marked like an old tortoise with mystic hieroglyphics upon the back!"   "The Affidavit."

But, in general, Melville's hieroglyphics move away from and not toward culture, away from art and toward nature, away from archaeology and toward raw gem. Eoliths are natural formations suggesting early Pleistocene pebble tools. Just as there is a moment between the living and inert, there is a moment neither clearly artifact nor clearly nature. The planet is littered with forms that intention will later seize.

Actual identification of man's earliest tools, however, is a matter of considerable difficulty, because obviously his first attempts at making tools from pieces of stone must have been all but indistinguishable from the accidents of nature. Indeed, naturally fractured stones probably served as the first implements. Even at the present time there are backward tribes who make use of convenient bits of sharp stone, sharks' teeth and shells as tools. Some Australian tribes occasionally chop trees and fashion wooden implements with naturally shaped pieces of stone selected by virtue of their sharp cutting edges.

Kenneth P. Oakley: *Man the Tool-Maker.*

In bony, ribby regions of the earth, where at the base of high broken cliffs masses of rock lie strewn in fantastic groupings upon the plain, you will often discover images as of the petrified forms of the Leviathan partly merged in the grass, which of a windy day breaks against them in a surf of green surges.

Then, again, in mountainous countries where the traveller is continually girdled by amphitheatrical heights; here and there from some lucky point of view you will catch passing glimpses of the profiles of whales defined along the undulating ridges.   "Of Whales in Paint."

It is evasive, yes, but it is never deformed beyond all recognition. Shape is battered, but basic congruence is sustained.

In life, the visible surface of the Sperm Whale is not the least among the many marvels he presents. Almost invariably it is all over obliquely crossed and re-crossed with numberless straight marks in thick array, something like those in the finest Italian line engravings. But these marks do not seem to be impressed upon the isinglass substance above mentioned, but seem to be seen through it, as if they were engraved upon the body itself. Nor is this all. In some instances, to the quick, observant eye, those linear marks, as in a veritable engraving, but afford the ground for far other delineations. These are hieroglyphical; that is, if you call those mysterious cyphers on the walls of pyramids hieroglyphics, then that is the proper word to use in the present connexion. By my retentive memory of the hieroglyphics upon one Sperm Whale in particular, I was much struck with a plate representing the old Indian character chiselled on the famous hieroglyphic palisades on the banks of the Upper Mississippi. Like those mystic rocks, too, the mystic-marked whale remains undecipherable. This allusion to the Indian rocks reminds me of another thing. Besides all the other phenomena which the exterior of the Sperm Whale presents, he not seldom displays the back, and more especially his flanks, effaced in great part of the regular linear appearance, by reason of numerous rude scratches, altogether of an irregular, random aspect. I should say that those New England rocks on the sea-coast, which Agassiz imagines to bear the marks of violent scraping contact with vast floating icebergs—I should say, that those rocks must not a little resemble the Sperm Whale in this particular. It also seems to me that such scratches in the whale are probably made by hostile contact with other whales; for I have most remarked them in the large, full-grown bulls of the species.

"The Blanket."

This passage contains some of the most central pairs in *Moby Dick*: Art-Nature; Soma-Hieroglyph; Violence of Creation-Violence of Mutilation; American Indian-Egyptian; Animal-Totem Animal; Whale-Indian; Accident-Intention; Appearance-Concealment; Prehistory-Archaeology. Hieroglyphics and teratology merge, with intelligence and planet-shaping; the Indians and whales of archaeology come alive in a moment that is so complicated and referential they might almost seem real—the remoteness of their existence as against the brilliance of the whale's surface; the scraping rocks of Agassiz; the Mississippian cultures. Occasionally one of the Bureau of American Ethnography Monographs will have an image as clear as this: some Hopi Indians painting themselves for the winter solstice ceremony; the facing page describing the rock strata, surface vegetation, and species of insects; turn the page to an explanation of house construction; and then the plate of a single hawk in profile, so black and white and dim every 1910 color stands out in the imagination of time. The following passages likewise from the Melville encyclopedia:

Champollion deciphered the wrinkled granite hieroglyphics. But there is no Champollion to decipher the Egypt of every man's and every being's face. Physiognomy, like every other human science, is but a passing fable. If then, Sir William Jones, who read in thirty languages, could not read the simplest peasant's face in its profounder and more subtle meanings, how may unlettered Ishmael hope to read the awful Chaldee of the Sperm Whale's brow?   "The Prairie."

A great pity, now, that this unfortunate whale should be harelipped. The fissure is about a foot across. Probably the mother during an important interval was sailing down the Peruvian coast, when earthquakes cause the beach to gape.   "The Righ Whale's head."

But still more curious was the fact of a lance-head of stone being found in him, not far from the buried iron, the flesh perfectly firm about it. Who had darted that stone lance? And when? It might have been darted by some Nor' West Indian long before America was discovered.

"The Pequod Meets the Virgin."

The ribs were hung with trophies; the vertebrae were carved with Arsacidean annals, in strange hieroglyphics; in the skull, the priests kept up an unextinguished aromatic flame, so that the mystic head again sent forth its vapory spout. . . "A Bower in the Arsacides."

3— The Contribution of the Whale to Depth Psychology

a— As Mammal

In Ferenczian psychology, the emergence of living creatures from the sea is considered a "catastrophe." The traumatic event of evolution has its ontogenetic parallel in birth, for the uterus is, foetally, the world ocean again. The "development of animal species with organs of copulation" (i.e., to reach the lost internal waters) is re-enacted, individually, in the "development of the primacy of the genital zone." Then the Ice Ages follow, bringing with them, ontogenetically, the adolescent latency period.[11]

The life cycle of the whale suggests both man's original exile and his possible redemption. The whales live in the oceanic waters, the womb from which man, in the phylogeny of the simpler land animals, has been banished (the newts to reach land, the reptiles to spawn there). But the whale was banished also! It returns only after the mammalian stage; it is not an original fish; it is a "man" who has somehow atoned for his sins (been cured of the neurosis).

> The cetaceans have reassumed the torpedo-like streamlined shape of primitive aquatic vertebrates; the body, however, is thick and rounded in section, and hence (unlike the typically slimmer fish) the main propulsive force is confined to the tail fin alone. As in other aquatic mammals, the tail has failed to resume its original fin structure, and, as in the sea cows, horizontal flukes supported by fibrous tissue supply the motive power. Usually in whales (as in ichthyosaurs) a fishlike dorsal fin has redeveloped. As in the sirenians, the hind legs are lost (except for internal rudiments), and the front limbs are steering flippers. Parallel, again, to the marine reptiles, extra joints may be added to the toes. Hair has been abandoned as a covering and may be absolutely lacking on the skin of the adult whale; a thick layer of fat—the blubber—affords insulation against the constant cold of the sea waters. . .
>
> Little is known of these two whale groups before the Miocene epoch. In the Eocene, however, archaic whales, the zeuglodonts, were already common in the seas. These were, in some cases, of considerable size (seventy feet is the apparent maximum), wih a body comparatively longer but slimmer than in later whales. . .Not improbably the whales have come from early creodont carnivores and have gradually taken up a fish-eating existence in the same way that later otters and seals have done. . .
>
> A.S. Romer: *Man and the Vertebrates.*

The uncanny similarity of whale to man was demonstrated dramatically when a whale became entangled in Wendell Seavey's fishing gear on Mount Desert Island and was dragged into shore. The fish-cutters were unable to handle it until Susan Seavey, a nurse, explained, on the basis of human anatomy, how it was to be cut up.

Melville's whale descriptions have this suggestion of a calm—no simple calm, but one which precedes all empires, even all hunting bands, which precedes everything man is. This is no doubt what modern whale-befrienders mean when they say they "communicate" with whales and learn things from them, things no human being could ever teach them. And perhaps Melville felt some of this pre-Western nurturing, tucked away in Typee with Fayaway, behind the tumult, down the nineteenth century evolutionary ladder. Whale pleasures are even more remote.

> Yes, we were now in that enchanted calm which they say lurks at the heart of every commotion. And still in the distracted distance we beheld the tumults of the outer concentric circles, and saw successive pods of whales, eight or ten in each, swiftly going round and round, like multiplied spans of horses in a ring; and so closely shoulder to shoulder, that a Titanic circus-rider might easily have overarched the middle ones, and so have gone round on their backs... Keeping at the centre of the lake, we were occasionally visited by small tame cows and calves; the women and children of this routed host...
>
> And thus, though surrounded by circle upon circle of consternations and affrights, did these inscrutable creatures at the centre freely and fearlessly indulge in all peaceful concernments; yea, serenely revelled in dalliance and delight. But even so, amid the tornadoed Atlantic of my being, do I myself still for ever centrally disport in mute calm; and while ponderous planets of unwaning woe revolve round me, deep down and deep inland there I still bathe me in eternal mildness of joy."
>
> "The Grand Armada"

b— As the Object of a Sado-Masochistic Hunt

The same whale for whom there exists sympathy as a mammal is the object of a vicious hunt. Melville writes of the whale nursery, but also gives recipes on the cooking of the whale. This contradiction ("all the food we eat is made of souls") I discussed in depth in Solar Journal: Oecological Sections, borrowing from Rasmussen's interviews with Eskimoes.[12] Totemic cultures understand that animals are ancestors of human beings and that a spirit animal takes revenge on humans for the use of its physical body. But, in a hostile spiritual and physical environment, man has little choice. The numbness prevails, and is ritualized, so that events take place totemically and ceremonially which would be abhorrent in isolation (no doubt eating of meat is itself such a ritual action for all who engage in it). "The Split Representation in the Art of Asia and America," under the title of which Lévi-Strauss writes about body-painting, masks, and mutilation, is also the schizophrenic split.[13] Alienation from reality is a cultural premise because any culture, in order to be itself, must be alienated from all other possibilities, including all other "humanities."

The Makah, for instance, kill a young boy in order to improve their whaling luck. The buoys and floats with which the hunt is conducted are puffed-up seal bladders. The whale is categorized and alienated from the provisions of mammalian mutual aid; it is divided, schematically, into blow-hole, eye, hump (taboo piece), flukes, strips around the carcass, creases, flipper, and tongue. Waterman writes: "The hide or pelt is stripped from the animal with as little cutting as possible. The head and front flippers are cut away and the body encircled about halfway down its length. The skin from the front half of the animal is then 'peeled off' in a forward direction, turning the hide inside out."[14] The whale could be a buffalo or a torture victim for the Plains Indian, putting us right back in the prairie and Parkman's *Oregon Trail* (how to cook and enjoy the hump). You can't say it's only a wooden whale, only a paper moon, but you do.

> Even a perfectly fresh whale stinks when he is opened. It is said that the man who first opens the carcass on the beach is sometimes overcome by the gasses, which burst out and 'cause him to faint.'[15]

Metcalf expands on the whole issue of sado-masochism in *Moby Dick* in his novel *Genoa*. The equivalent of nineteenth century whale-ship violence a century later is war crimes, rape, kidnapping, murder, the teratology of XXY chromosomes, and extreme psychiatric methodology, as lobotomy and shock treatment. I will not discuss this comparison here because I have written on it at length in my essay on Paul Metcalf in *the Book of Being Born Again into the World*.[16] The cultural obsession which makes the cosmic aspect of *Moby Dick* more extreme and concrete in twentieth century terms translates the psychoanalytic into criminal insanity, genetic and somatic manipulation, and anthropological awareness of the structural nature of totemic violence, all of which are more literal, in terms of language and brain physiology, than the traumas and mutilations of *Moby Dick*. Melville approaches the consciousness of, say, Brakhage's "The Act of Seeing with One's Own Eyes" (the film of the Pittsburgh morgue) most closely by his own dissections of the whale.[17]

c— As General Depth-Psychology Guinea Pig

Melville intuited the kind of "time-depth" in illness and birth-trauma that would later be the mainstay of Reichian therapy, scientology, and gestalt. Where a psychoanalytic mode measures depth-in-time by symptomology and nervous impediment, Melville stuck to stellar, geographical, and Tertiary scales. The diagnosis is the same.

The sea-dwelling mammal of Melville's desire for rebirth and end to exile is replaced, in current imagery, with the overall possibility of therapy. The visionary image of the whale becomes a case history, and the potential artist never "indulges" his psychotic intuitions. The whole occasion is, again, more literal, perhaps more humane, but also terrifically depleted. Melville's "psychological novel" does not foreshadow the modern masterpieces of the genre but instead the therapies themselves, the radical psychoanalytic arts of a more desperate time (the same time that has come to the end of the whales and thus must make its false and hopeless venture at the stars). In that sense, the *Moby Dick* that is not the forerunner of Tennessee Williams or J.D. Sallinger *is* the forerunner of Reich's *Cosmic Superimposition*. Exactly those galaxies alive even as they are stars (stars even as they are the source of human sexual energy). The nostalgia Melville feels for whales Reich feels for the sky.

> Outside, a child is a child, an infant is an infant, and a mother is a mother, no matter whether in the form of a deer, or a bear, or a human being... Outside, to know the stars is to know God, and to meditate about God is to meditate about the heavens. Inside, somehow, if you believe in God, you do not understand or you refuse to understand the stars. Outside, if you search in the heavens, you refuse, and rightly so, to believe in the sinfulness of the natural embrace. Outside, you feel your blood surging and you do not doubt that something is moving in you, a thing you call your emotion, with its location undoubtedly in the middle of your body and close to your heart. Inside, you do not live with your total organism, but only with your brain... there is only empty space and atoms dissolved into an endless row of 'particles'..." [18]

C— The Etymological

Although Melville's "whale" has few literary kin, its ethnographic and mythological forerunners are abundant. It is Buffon's snake Foucault describes in *Words and Things*:

> When one has the story of an animal to tell, it is useless and impossible to choose between the role of the naturalist and that of an anthologist: in one and the same form of knowledge must be gathered all that has been *seen* and *heard*, all that has been related by nature or by men in the language of the world, of tradition, or of poets. To know a beast, or a plant, or anything from the earth, is to collect the whole thick layer of signs that have been deposited in them or on them; it is to recover also all the constellations of forms when they take on the characteristic of emblems. [19]

Its complex mixture of totemic and descriptive characteristics is implied in the "six-dimensionality" of American Indian sculpture:

> Fins, ears, and feet often take the form of birds' heads. The fact that eye and joint designs are indistinguishable makes this possible. The claws of a foot, or the curve of a flipper, become the beak of the bird whose eye is suggested by the joint design. The joints of the two shoulders become the eyes of a face which fills the body area, provided with ears, mouth, and nose. The well-known salmon-trout's-head and double-eye designs are merely elaborations of ovoids into facelike patterns. The famous "Rain Wall" at Klukwan is literally covered with over fifty such extraneous faces, many of them fitted out with little bodies, arms, and legs. The tails of whales are often elaborated into faces because of the similarity of the fluke designs to ears.   Bill Holm: *Northwest Coast Indian Art.*

Its sociological distortion is recalled by Lévi-Strauss' ethnozoology and structural myth:

> Thanks to the transformation illustrated in the Opaye myth, we can resolve the apparent contradiction by isolating those features that remain invariable at the level of the set.[20]

Melville's Cetology is not pure taxonomy. It is, in part, a satire of the strained precision of classificatory terminology. No doubt part of his original plan, before the book on whales merged with the adventure story, was to write a philosophical and amusing account of the whale kingdom, a carry-over from the colloquies of *Mardi*. There is ample material on whale physiology, the technology of whaling, the cooking of whale meat, the whale in history and archaeology, famous whales, artistic whales, star whales, and even incompletely developed whale-like events.

> At some old gable-roofed country houses you will see brass whales hung by the tail for knockers to the road-side door. When the porter is sleepy, the anvil-headed whale would be best. But these knocking whales are seldom remarkable as faithful essays. On the spires of some old-fashioned churches you will see sheet-iron whales placed there for weathercocks; but they are so elevated and beside that are to all intents and purposes so labelled with "*Hands off!*" you cannot examine them closely enough to decide upon their merit.   "Of Whales in Paint."

Moby Dick opens not with: "Call me Ishmael," as if often remembered by readers, but with the "Etymology (supplied by a late consumptive usher to a grammar school)" and the "Extracts (supplied by a sub-sub-librarian)." The irony is intentional, but not only as mockery. By citing his sources in a playful manner, Melville calls attention to their human quality and the very personal research that follows. The book begins with the same curious tension between absolute fact and human notation that continues throughout.

139

The etymology introduces "Whale" as a word before the book introduces the whale itself. We are given the three major Indo-European derivations (epitomized by the Latin Cetus, the Danish Hvalt, and the Spanish Ballena); hence, the roots for the words Cetology, Whale, and Baleen. The word Whale is explored in terms of the different contexts of its etymology, including the senses of roundness and rolling, or wallowing, plus the connotation of arching and vaultedness. What would seem to be informed by a purely historical interest in language actually sharpens our earliest sense of the real whale. As the phonemics change, giving different perspectives on the origins of names for this being, the being rolls through them and survivies them all. The whale is the only link. The first implication is that the whale has evolved and changed with culture, from fishing to farming to urban civilization; underlying that is the sense that the whale is difficult to name, i.e., difficult to receive into history.

The real impact of the Etymology comes in the last two entries, the Pekee-Nuee-Nuee of Fegee and the Pehee-Nuee-Nuee of Erromangoan. The ethnographic frame does a flip, and we find ourselves in a different language system. The whale attains phonemic representation in the native Pacific, in terms of a unique heap of morphology, semantics, word-formation, sound-drift, mythology, synchronous event, etc., in a system that is cut off from ours *before* the common sighting of a whale. There is an Erromangoan whale never seen by those on the *Pequod*, roughly conceived in *Moby Dick*, that is part of the absolute condition of present things. The whale, as *Moby Dick* attempts to enclose it in its own waters, is in existence under different names, throughout the globe, and retains an existential realness even as it is torn from cosmology to cosmology.

The Extracts themselves are Biblical, Classical, historical, ecological, economic, mythological, comical, apocryphal. Sometimes the mentality of the sub-sub-librarian prevails, and an extract is banal and pedantic. In other cases, the teratologist prevails, and the whale comes from a book of wonders. They are sequentially arranged, and run full-speed into the narrative: "Ten or fifteen gallons of blood are thrown out of the heart at a stroke, with immense velocity," followed by: "The aorta of a whale is larger in the bore than the main pipe of the water-works at London Bridge, and the water roaring in its passage through that pipe is inferior in impetus and velocity to the blood gushing from the whale's heart." The former is from John Hunter's Account of the Dissection of a Whale and the latter from Paley's Theology. A sub-series within the extracts gives a continuity of historically significant whale references, including: "Now the Lord had prepared a great fish to swallow up Jonah!" and "Whales in the sea/God's voice obey" (N.E. Primer). The comical and metaphorical Extracts fall together:

"Spain—a great whale stranded on the shores of Europe" (Edmund Burke. (Somewhere.)) and ". . . and the breath of the whale is frequently attended with such an insupportable smell, as to bring on a disorder of the brain" (Ulloa's South America).

They close with a haunting Whale Song:

> Oh, the rare old Whale, mid storm and gale
> In his ocean home will be
> A giant in might, where might is right,
> And King of the boundless sea.

As the last notes of this song are still in our ears, and all of Western history echoing behind them, the title page turns and: "Call me Ishmael."

D— The Pacific

To Melville, the Atlantic-Pacific is one world ocean, but its Atlantic element is Euro-American and commercial. West of America is the unsettled world ocean, of indefinite extent, filled with exotic races of men, unknown flora and fauna. The Mediterranean of the *Odyssey* is the Atlantic of *The Tempest* is the Pacific of *Moby Dick*.

Let us put Melville's nineteenth century version next to the Pacific of twentieth century California. It is like the difference between San Francisco and not, i.e., no difference at all, except for the mist.

> The same waves wash the moles of the new-built California towns, but yesterday planted by the recentest race of men, and lave the faded but still gorgeous skirts of Asiatic lands, older than Abraham; while all between float milky-ways of coral isles, and low-flying, endless, unknown Archipelagoes, and impenetrable Japans. Thus the mysterious, divine Pacific zones the worlds whole bulk about; makes all coasts one bay to it; seems the tide-beating heart of the earth. Lifted by those eternal swells, you needs must own the seductive god, bowing your head to Pan.
> "The Pacific."

I do not know how to describe Pacific. Charles Fort once claimed that space ships passed continually over the earth and dropped their debris upon it: fish in the dry prairies, tadpoles in the Sahara, black snow in Tahiti, bloody rain, shreds of life, unknown metals. That is what Pacific is like. The debris of culture rains down upon it, collects here as if at the bottom of a bowl. These troubled adolescents and adults seem drawn or blown here by the slant of the times: dazed pilgrims, disenchanted and dispossessed. They might be the long-lost children of the Pequod's motley crew waiting patiently on a forgotten isle for Moby Dick to appear again. For the last few months the school has shared its quarters with a traveling commune, but now the commune has moved on, leaving behind those too lame or stoned to travel. They drift like abandoned ghosts through the school: pale barefoot women with weeping children, a long-robed religious fanatic claiming to be God, a demented ex-Marine who puts his fist through windows while shouting about money. Even now, as I write, I can see from my window two visitors who arrived a few days ago. One is a bearded and burly man in his fifties whom God converted in a dream from selling stocks to begging for his living like a Zen priest. The other is the girl he has found somewhere: a skinny teen-ager who laughs continually to herself and dances up and down the dirt roads continuing dementedly with unseen spirits, bobbing her head at their words, and smoking a thin cigar.

There is something grotesque and touching about it all, as there always is about those who try to create for themselves what culture has denied them. It is a bit like the Pacific cargo-cult, an absurd reconstruction of community with only one aim in mind: to magically attract the gods and grace we want but do not understand. I remember now a scene from Eisenstein's Ten Days That Shook the World. In a barren landscape hundreds of huge barrels were set into the ground, and in them lived thousands of dwarfs and freaks, and when the revolution began they emerged howling from their barrels to join the fight. This is how Pacific seems to me. Here are the barrels and dwarfs, but the revolution has not yet begun, may never begin, and this is what happens in the meantime.

Peter Marin: *In A Man's Time.*

1— A Historical Chronicle

1500 B.C.   Furthest extent of Egyptian Empire into Western Asia.

1200 B.C.   "Helen/said Herodotus,/was only the last/of the European girls/to be absconded with/by the Asiatics/   for which read/ Phoenician sailors."   Olson.

1000 B.C.   Beginning of Assyrian Empire.

800 B.C.   Phoenician trade expeditions to Brazil.

500 B.C.   "Man is estranged from that which is most familiar."

Heraclitus.

0 A.D.   Roman Empire; Mediterranean civilization.

100 A.D.   Huns chased from China, begin march toward Europe.

350 A.D.   Julian allows Franks to settle within borders of Roman Empire in exchange for military service.

400 A.D.   Barbarians defend Roman Empire; ask to be accepted as Romans.

500 A.D.   Clovis unites Franks, is converted to Christianity.

550 A.D.	Fugitives of Rome set up merchant republic of Venice; their first industries are fishing and refining of sea salt.
600 A.D.	Lombards conquer Italy, separate Byzantium from the Roman Empire.
650 A.D.	Muslim conquest of Persian Empire, plus Syrian and Eygptian provinces of Byzantine Empire; this marks the end of the Hellenized Asia of Alexander the Great. Swedes set up trade routes in Russia between Baltic and Caspian and from the Gulf of Finland to the Volga, linking the Baltic to the Black Sea; Irish Christians settle in Iceland, Northern Gaul, Germany.
700 A.D.	Muslim invasion of Africa; Visigoths retake Spain from Byzantium.
750 A.D.	Establishment of Carolingian line in Europe.
800 A.D.	Slav penetration into Europe stopped at the Elbe and Saale Rivers; Norse landings in England; Vikings in Iceland.
850 A.D.	Carolingian Empire begins to dissipate into modern boundaries of France, Germany, Italy, Belgium, Switzerland, Spain; Roman villages become mediaeval baronies run by seigneurs; apportionment of woods, meadows, and marshes; building of local mills; no commerce; self-sufficient agriculture; Danish invasion of England; Norse invasion of Ireland.
900 A.D.	Alfred the Great abandons England east of London to the Norse; other Norse invade Lisbon, Seville, Italy; Magyars invade eastern Europe; Arabs conquer Sicily; beginning of Russian-Swedish state under Olaf; replacement of general Roman system of calculation with regional systems of weights and measurements; Irish in New World.
1000 A.D.	Trapped between the hypothetical millennium and the premature vision of economic revival, Gerbert, the Pope, studied Pythagoras, music, geometry, requested Arabic mathematical tables. He constructed a plain globe of wood on which he marked the spots where the stars rise and set, with supporting armillary globes showing their courses across the sky; Otto III, pupil of Gerbert, attempted to reunite Germania and Rome, but the Alps, bisecting a new north-south plane, threw this plan into obscurity. Vikings in North America; a polar bear is shipped to the Sultan of Egypt.

1050 A.D.   Norman state in southern Italy: in 1066: in England.

1100 A.D.   Major European coins are Saracen gold pieces, often with Allah rubbed off them (Arabic lettering remains); Islam controls all passages in time and space to Indo-European origins on the Mediterranean; First Crusade: Christians conquer Jerusalem.

1150 A.D.   Merchant class in the cities of Europe; clearing of the forests; charters; Dikes of Flanders; re-opening of European mines and striking of gold and silver coins; Pisa and Genoa rival Venice as cities trading between Europe and Near East; Byzantine libraries ignored; Kingdom of Jerusalem falls.

1200 A.D.   Mediterranean trade to Europe re-opened; Basque cod-fishery in North Atlantic; Genghis Kahn in Asia; Viking villages in Greenland visited by merchant ships from Norway.

1300 A.D.   Marco Polo in China; trade fairs in Europe; Genoese and Portuguese explorations in the Atlantic.

1350 A.D.   Black Death; mining of gold in England; Genoese explorations of Canary Islands; Biscayans aid French in Hundred Years' War with England.

1400 A.D.   Last Norwegian ship to visit Greenland; Henry the Navigator (of Portugal) initiates voyages along the shore of Africa.

1439 A.D.   Sheep placed on seven Azore Islands by the Portuguese; printing press in Europe; Inca Empire in Peru.

1488 A.D.   Dias rounds Cape of Good Hope (Africa circled, pointing East); Fuggers invest in German mines, inland base of German power; Bristol fishermen in the New World, catching and rack-drying cod; last Greenland settlers absorbed into Eskimo culture.

So what is 1492 the date for? And the answer is: for combining the two Europa-centric visions of the world: One Europe grounded in the old Mediterranean with lingering hopes of restoring the Roman Empire (or at least the Roman cosmology), reaching out for trade with Asia, regaining specie power, starting up trade fairs and markets, flat linear world, Christian, resetting boundaries by force more than half a millennium after Verdun (into World Wars I and II): this is the Europe of the counter-reformation (later), King Philip of Spain, De Soto and his ravages of Southeastern Indian civilization, Cortez, Napoleon (even that late, with the sale of Louisiana, the one strategic land he held). Then there is the Europe grounded in the old Atlantic: Druid, the gods of Eig and Muck, fishermen of Biscay and Bristol, hermeticists, Stonehenge relics, Cretean and Basque descendants, White Goddess quest, Irish priest-voyages, pagan, round world, open astral-Egyptian cosmology, secret maps and routes, lost civilizations, trading with Vinland as with Africa, globally oriented, Brasil a hot wind on its breath even before the solid landstrike of South America. This is the Europe of Shakespeare's *Tempest*, John Dee, John Smith, Homer, Hesiod, the Greek-Atlantean Empire, the Norse Sagas, Hamlet's mill, the Persian *Book of Kings*, the *Kalevala*, the reindeer scapula, and the Arabic taxonomies and encyclopedias.[21]

Columbus didn't discover anything. The Irish, the Norse, the English, the Portuguese, had been there before. And everyone knew it. The Portuguese had qualified navigators in the Azores and Madeiras; Genoa itself had visited the Canaries and sought ports beyond; the Norse knew America and had abandoned it; the English had clear fixes on the fishing grounds, and their maps, if never published, circulated in Bristol. Why would anyone advertise good cod shoals? Of course, these nations laughed at Columbus; he was selling something they already had and he didn't. So he sold it to Spain who, ignorant even then of the Basques as she was of the qabbalists, got what they paid for: a menially literal invention of a foreign slave-trade gold-mine land. What was already in their imagination Columbus found for them (and we remember him yet because it has stayed such in our imagination of it). He lied for ten years and had the Spanish navy and bastard aristocracy running around after his ambiguously self-serving pranks, and killed off most of the native Indians doing it. Columbus was backward enough and forward enough, stubborn enough to discover America so that it stayed discovered (and yet unaware of it in his lifetime); he purposely omitted from his report the great Mayan ships headed for the Mississippi, filled with trade goods. He didn't want to see that.[22] Others found the old Atlantic and used it for its incredible fertility (twice that of the European soil), but Columbus found it in the Spanish mind, and Spain, with the Pope as ally, made it part of Rome, took it from the Algonquian-Skraeling and gave it to Pizarro-Cortez.

What Columbus did was bring the two Europes together: round world and flat world, pagan and Christian, lost India and unknown Amerindia the same ancient lineage, secret trade maps and unknown kingdoms and mythologies fused with public grants and acknowledged sources, private fishing grounds placed in the European domain, pagan gold and Spanish gold identified as the same specie(s), legendary Brasil and the blessed isles wedged into the profane space of European expansion; the occult, with its alien tribes and ceremonies, sacked for visible presence (for Columbus

145

simply made visible, made it impossible for it to be invisible anymore: what everyone was already staring at). If Columbus did not discover America, he discovered imperialism as a geocosmic mode and lost forever the Homeric sea and its wondrous peoples. Beyond the Atlantic of Columbus lies the prairie of Cooper and the highways, Route 66, Route 44, Interstate 80, from the Atlantic to the Pacific. America is nothing but a long trade route, an artery, catching what falls off the trucks. For all our Eastward pushing, this is all we have of the East.

Melville was an accidental visionary like Columbus. He joined the Pacific to the Atlantic; he found the Pacific.

He connected the new Pacific of cargo cults, totem beasts, sorcerers, and native women to the old Atlantic-Mediterranean of commerce, migration, Christian settlement, and closed villages. He didn't discover the Pacific, but he made it visible in terms of what we already knew, made it happen that new information crowded ports already shut into the old travellers' tales, the old cosmology. He reached almost to primordial Asia.

Moby Dick is Columbus' journey again; Paul Metcalf makes us believe this in *Genoa.*[23] Melville crossed that same confused psycho-geography, ended up in the identical India-Indian madhouse. Three-hundred-and-fifty-nine years later Melville restores the battered space in which Columbus made his stride—across which: morning shone in a qabbalistic dream (later Borges in Argentina, Spicer in San Francisco), as much as any sea-islands Cabot or the Corte Real Brothers saw. And later, *Don Quixote,* back into the continent. The birds and gulls, raw and wild species Champlain found on the outer rocks of a continent, Columbus did not see, not feathers and dung, not Indian mounds and domesticated corn; these birds of Columbus were like geese on the margins of landfall, nursery rhyme birds, nonsense syllables in a backward reading of Europe. But Melville got into the real islands, and opened the world ocean for North America; in so doing he passed Columbus and recovered what could be left, in Nantucket Harbor and Virginia, of the old cosmology. As surely as sun on strands of algae and flying fish. And he may have been a blind visionary, but he was no fool of the occasion he had touched.

> . . . though we know the sea to be an everlasting terra incognita, so
> that Columbus sailed over numberless unknown worlds to discover his one
> superficial western one. . .   'Brit."

E— The Techno-Economic

Whaling was the oil industry in Melville's time, and to forget that catching and draining a whale was like digging and tapping an oil well is to turn the ledgers of Aramco into an E.M. Forester romance. The containedness of the whale as compared to the vastness of an oil-field is not a relevant issue in an age when oil-fields were unknown and cities were smaller and uses of oil fewer.

Furthermore, the whaleship was a whole socio-economic stratum in nineteenth century America. Those men were on the ship for the same reasons that men now, from the ghettoes, enlist in the army, run numbers rackets, and start cocaine rings. They were hobos, seekers of fortune, misfits (from the rural out-districts of Maine, Vermont, and Kentucky). Note Browne's *Etchings of a Whaling Cruise*, especially Chapter III, subtitled: "Yankee Mack" and "Voracity of the Portuguese." The whaleboat was a slum, a trade union, Crusaders, and a factory. Even as the ship travelled to the edge of Western cosmology, its social order touched the radical boundaries of American possibility (an aspect the social idealists chose to interpret as nascent democracy, but which I take as either social geography or economic anthropology). It was simply a matter of earning a living, feeding the small domestic industry with fuel, and keeping body and soul together (fallen "nobility," such as H.M. and J.F. Cooper, thrown in with the Rockefellers of following decades). If it was perilous, it had advantages that working in a plutonium factory in 1975 doesn't. And if Herman felt an invisible radiation at sea, that was his own dread insight, and was a bare tremor then in American economic life.

The whaleship was a crowded city street in summer time: a noise which Melville lets through like a sudden rush or din in certain chapters, reminiscent of the Shakesperian scenes staged for the London street folk in the pits. But they also give a sense of just how much noise there is, and thus increase the pure density of the book. It is as though flashes of the night sky, full with stars and Milky Way, were thrown onto the stock market floor every now and then to let people know the Big Show in which they are playing out their lots. Conversely, the cosmic perspective, the sheer epic constellation of *Moby Dick*, is broken by voices and rumbles from the social, economic, political, and ethnic galaxies. Or, how this single ship, despite its illuminations from Plato, Spinoza, Marquesan shamanism, etc., is completely bound to the sociology of its time. Even the plutonium leak in the factory will end up in the reality streets of some poor Okie town. Which is what Ahab takes with him over the brink.

> "Um, um, um. Stop that thunder! Plenty too much thunder up here. What's the use of thunder? Um, um, um. We don't want thunder; we want rum; give us a glass of rum. Um, um, um!"
> "Midnight Aloft. Thunder and Lightning."

Melville's Christianity has a certain relevance here, at least as an insight into his need to create a non-Christian world, a world made up of pagans and Christians essentially outside Christianity (beginning with Ishmael's joining Queequeg in worship). Like the collapsing surface of the star, Christianity's implosion releases the pagan energies that have been contained within it from Oriental and Saxon beginnings: those which it gathered into itself to make Rome again, and those which it must take aboard the whaleship to people an industrial society. This proletariat reality allows Melville to set a philosophical opus in a blasphemous circumstance: lower class, working world, and savage. It is clear from the beginning that *Moby Dick* is a book that is going to go to church and give the sermon, but Herman wants to make sure that the sermon is heard out on the streets. *Moby Dick* is the debut for numerous unknown radicals, revolutionaries, millenarians, heathen spies, and devil-worshippers, who were populating America all along without fair due. He does not present them to admonish the wayward. His target is the righteous, and there were enough of those in his own family alone. So it is simultaneously social criticism, pop art, and sociology, and its counterparts are to be found in the ethnographies of the time: how the Kwakiutl make a canoe. Or the Seminole build a house. Or to list the cast as it is given ("Midnight, Forecastle"):

> Nantucket sailor, Dutch sailor, French sailor, Pip, Iceland sailor, Maltese sailor, Sicilian sailor, Long-Island sailor, Azore sailor, China sailor, Tashtego, Old Manx sailor, Lascar sailor, Tahitan sailor, Portuguese sailor, Danish sailor, English sailor, Daggoo, Spanish sailor, St. Jago's sailor, Belfast sailor.

> OLD MANX SAILOR. Ready formed. There! the ringed horizon. In that ring Cain struck Abel. Sweet work, right work! No? Why then, God, mad'st thou the ring?

Straight back to the importance of the whaling industry, which Melville gives right off: "... yearly consuming 4,000,000 of dollars; the ships worth, at the time of sailing, $20,000,000; and every year importing into our harbors a well reaped harvest of $7,000,000." "The Advocate."

And Olson covers this in *Call Me Ishmael:*

> We forget the part the chase of the whale played in American economy. It started from a shortage of fats and oils. The Indian had not cattle, the colonist not enough. It was the same with pigs and goats. Red and white alike had to use substitutes. It accounts for the heavy slaughter of the passenger pigeon and the curlew, plentiful birds; and the slaughter of the buffalo.

> The Indians appear to have taken shore whales from an early time. The Makahs around Cape Flattery knew tricks only the present day Norwegian whalers have applied. They blew up seal skins to slow the run of a wounded whale like a sea anchor and to float the dead whale when heavier than water.

. . . . .

COMBUSTION. All whales yield oil. Most of the oil is a true fat, a glyceride of the fatty acids. Unlike the Indians the settlers did not find it edible. They boiled the blubber down for tallow. In addition to this fat, commonly called whale oil, the sperm whale and the bottle-nose yield a solid wax called spermaceti and a liquid wax called sperm oil. The spermaceti wax is contained in the cavity of the head (vide chp. "Cistern and Buckets," *Moby-Dick*), and in the bones.

Economic historians, lubbers, fail to heft the industry in American economic life up to the Civil War. (In 1859 petroleum was discovered in Pennsylvania. Kerosene, petroleum, and paraffin began rapidly to replace whale oil, sperm oil, and spermaceti wax as illuminating oil, lubricants, and raw materials for candles.)

Whaling expanded at a time when agriculture not industry was the base of labor and when foreign not domestic commerce was the base of trade.

F— Star, Trauma, Etymology, Pacific, Oil

If we try to bring all of these together, we come up with a complex metaphysical tale whose elegance is far less than the simple intensity at the core of *Moby Dick*. In order to find a contemporary parallel just to the voyage of the *Pequod*, we would have to imagine something like a super-tanker trying to wedge and thread its way through the Northwest Passage, or a mammoth rocket ship en route to Jupiter to harvest the Earth's annual supply of natural gas. Perhaps a Moon-voyage, whose primary aim is to bring back raw materials scarce on Earth and whose secondary aim is to discover the origin of the planetary system. Or a longer star-flight in which the connection with Earth is telepathic and across time-dilation. But these have to be real, lower class, and only, without technological alleviation, and that may now be impossible for a long time. Clearly, Melville seized these things right at the horizon, and the fact that the book cannot be done over makes it all the more pressing for us to take it as it is.

FOOTNOTES

This essay was compiled from notes handed out to my classes while teaching *Moby Dick* at Goddard College. The original course was in the fall of 1972. The notes were expanded when the course was taught again in the fall of 1974. Additional material was added during rewritings in 1975 and 1976. The footnotes are abbreviated, as they were compiled without access to the library from which the piece was written.

[1] This tape was made from a reading and Melville lecture Olson gave at Goddard College, Plainfield, Vermont, probably sometime in late 1962. The quote itself is an aside Olson made after reading the Milton Stern section from "Equal, That Is, To The Real Itself."

[2] "Equal, That Is, To The Real Itself."

[3] Harper and Brothers published the first edition of *Moby-Dick* in 1851, but the new paperback edition makes one think they discovered it yesterday, along with everyone else.

[4] Claude Lévi-Strauss: *The Raw and the Cooked.* The point I am making here will seem strained or poetic unless one is familiar with the subtleties of Lévi-Strauss' system, especially as they involve the transition from culture to nature and back. The totemic element of *Moby Dick* is particularly adaptable to that system, and the whale comes clearer in the context of *The Raw and the Cooked* than it does in terms of any straight "natural" history.

[5] *ibid.,* in direct continuation.

[6] from Olson's reading at Goddard. Otherwise-unpublished sections of this reading appear in *Io*/16, Earth Geography Booklet #4, Anima Mundi, Winter Issue, 1972-73.

[7] "is there anything/to the possibility/that some of the non-Euclidean/roughnesses are here/involved—Hittite, or Hurrian/may not be the only evidences,/there may be East African/—and again what about Libyan?"

[8] "Goethe's View of Nature and the World of Science and Technology," in *Across the Frontiers*, Harper Torchbook, 1975.

[9] See *Io*/17, *Poems and Glyphs* by Charles Stein; page 15.

[10] Claude Lévi-Strauss: *The Raw and the Cooked;* Figure 15, comparing native and European constellations.

[11] Sandor Ferenczi: *Thalassa.*

[12] Black Sparrow, Los Angeles, 1970; written in 1967-8.

[13] Claude Lévi-Strauss: *Structural Anthropology.*

[14] T.T. Waterman: *The Whaling Equipment of the Makah Indians.*

[15] *ibid.*

[16] North Atlantic Books, Plainfield, Vermont, 1974; written in 1971-2.

[17] See *Io*/14, Earth Geography Booklet #3, Imago Mundi, Summer, 1972, "Interview with Stan Brakhage;" beginning page 357.

[18] Wilhelm Reich: *Cosmic Superimposition.*

[19] Michel Foucault: "The Writing of Things." For full text, see *Io/5*, Doctrine of Signatures, Summer, 1968.

[20] Claude Lévi-Strauss: *The Raw and the Cooked*; this quote precedes and is continuous with the other two, which is why it is chosen here.

[21] The argument is synthesized from *Northern Mists* by Carl Sauer and *Hamlet's Mill* by Giorgio de Santillana and Hertha von Dechend.[24]

[22] "The pillage of the trading canoe gave a preview of an extensive and elaborate native commerce, in this instance between Central Mexico and the Gulf of Honduras. The cargo was being brought from the west and some of it came from distant parts. The cotton goods may have been from Yucatán. The tools and weapons of yellowish obsidian were from central Mexico, also the marble or alabaster, known as Mexican onyx. The copper bells and good copper axes indicate Michoacán as source. The kernels that served as coins were cacao beans, produced mainly on the Pacific coast. . .

The landfall at Guanaja Island and the land on the adjacent mainland were the first European contact with any of the high cultures of the New World, which later were found to extend north as far as Rió Pánuco. Possibly Columbus had a glimmering of such a culture when he identified the new coast with Champa of Indochina. He did not follow it up nor did he tarry here or have any inclination to return. The discovery was not appreciated at the time, and had no bearing on the later conquest of New Spain." Carl Sauer: *The Early Spanish Main.*

[23] Paul Metcalf: *Genoa, A Telling of Wonders.*

[24] Frances Yates gives a picture of these two Europes by contrasting them in her description of John Dee's library in *Theatre of the World:*

"The whole Renaissance is in this library. Or rather it is the Renaissance as interpreted by Ficino and Pico della Mirandola, with its slant towards philosophy, science, and magic, rather than towards purely grammarian humanist studies. It is a Renaissance without doctrinal ferocity, either Reformation or Counter Reformation, but with very strong mystical and magical leanings, a Renaissance which prefers to read of the hierarchies of angels with Pseudo-Dionysius (well represented in the library) than the works of Calvin. And it is a Renaissance situated in England, with its characteristic development of popular science with a strong practical bent, with an outlook towards navigation and the sea, and new lands beyond the sea, a Renaissance which includes in its historical studies the British History of Geoffrey of Monmouth (represented in the library) and the chronicles of England, a Renaissance which values poetry, ancient and modern, Greek and Latin, Italian and French."

My argument here, and in the essay, is not that Herman Melville is an inheritor of John Dee's Europe, but that he, like Columbus, succeeded, unconsciously, in realigning two sympathetic traditions. Because of the public prejudices of Western thought, such a joining must always come from revelations of hermetic, geographical, and cosmic lore in the context of general humanism and state theology. It can never be the other way. The more ancient, remnant Europe stands forever in an archetypal relationship to modernism, hidden from it, yet powerfully determining its course.

If Columbus is the dark winter solstice Astarte of this marriage, using it for dismemberment and impotence, Melville is its bright summer solstice Demeter, bringing from it wisdom and rebirth.

Donald F. Wellman

The Pool

The sag
    where the sky weighs
      on the roof of an abandoned boathouse
The Pool makes a stomach to the island
the small mouth digests and expells
Horses would haul the boats from the yards
        onto the mudflats
Fish Point
    what remains are a cellar and an appletree
And Ocean, continually
        enters and withdraws from The Pool
    As the water comes closer
    the mud churns and the thumb
with the forefinger or opposite point
      gropes for the prey
My back's bent in the digging for clams
And the hods force my arms to earth
Above the high-water line, the refuse
      of bleached shell
        rusted nails, rope, broken bottles
    arrowheads cover the gray sand
The leaves of beach spinach
to add to the salad

The Heath-Stepper

A cold wind owns the heath
Frost weights each blade of sedge

Footprints trace a path
across clumps of bog turf
Ice
the coldest seed
shags the fern
The heartbeat slows

––––––––––

The hand that knots water
at times
untwists the threads
at times
takes charcoal and rubs

A winter-killed deer
Time rots the gray marrow

––––––––––

In a root-tangled bone-heap of stumps
washed ashore
I kindle the bonfire for all that will
be coals

The Wait

As long fingers braid the clouds
The tide crawls over mudflats
mixes in pools
Sand, gravel, pieces of shell
The waxy corner of a milk carton
wets through a sack
The slow dissolving of fibers
A memory of the process
Clam-worms, tunnels in the mud
A hook of sun seems to touch
the western mountain
A smell of rust, of iron rails
discolors my palms

—2—

The edges darken as the tear opens
The sack drifts under the slow waves

A punt cuts between mooring ropes
The rowers back to the shore

The prows of lobster boats
in from the day's hauling
point toward the island

—3—

The schedule of changes
describes columns of minutes and hours
against holes or islands in time

I search the far waves
for the core of a permanent myth
I do not wear a watch
No boats move on the open water

A chain, the texture, almost orange fur
drapes over stones and curls into mud
where near waves isolate a granite block

As eyes abstract the necessary objects/
The process of watching provides coherence

—OR—   (month/day/year do not grid
            (the distances the mind holds

According to legend   / The sharply defined bulk
the earth lowers itself   / of the western mountain
into the night tunnels   /
and this process   / moves nearer in the eye
outlasts all waiting   / as the island falls away

—4—

Maps and calendars were invented
to ease the longing
for systems of marking off

—BUT— (To complete the work begun with clouds/
              to attempt what intellection requires:

The science of watching gives eyes
The strength to pull
The tense thread
of the horizon where the island
bobs

—5—

DO EYES MAKE LAND ? ——————— Otherwise: the wait
                                           for the event
                                         will outlast
Mindful eyes   awareness
take the gray
powder that adheres
to the lowest tier of blocks   *Arrival—*needs—*Departure*
to build the solid grid
of the retaining wall

The hands need the iron rail
to support their idle weight

John Thorpe

Harriet

Time is—
as far as I know
the only stroke on my brain control—
which to *me*
seems permanently damaged.
Whether this is last week
or next I cannot

remember.
I miss blue sky hues
and feel under a bowl
of white.
I do not think corn stalks look as tall
as in dryer air.
The maple trees
which seem to reach up into the sky

are getting spots of gold—
reflecting sunshine across the room
The maples turning yellow
tell me they are soft—
not hard maples.

I have been alone in the cozy sunroom
knitting a scarf—
for Red Cross to send to Russia.
It could be used for a girl
to tie around her head going to school.

We live in the small glass room
windows on 3 sides—
on hinges so as many as we like
can be opened,
as the whole place is screened.
It is where we live—as trees
keep out most of direct sun
& Street is so wide
no one can look in—

It is almost like facing a Park
                    shaded by *tall* maples—

The bureau in my room
is made of rosewood
& has glass knobs on the drawers
Half way across the top
is a long box
with cover on hinges
to keep toilet articles in.

A stiff southwest wind is playing
w/ the elms so that I feel in the woods
                    Our elms are dark green.
                    & Another kind is light green.

There was plenty of land when this city
                    started & east of the Webster farm
                    I have counted 9 ditches
                        now dry
            wch in my childhood contained clear water
            and from wch anyone cd drink.

In this room is an old-fashioned chair
                    like one my father had—
            There is also a small round table.
        At each end of the room is a radiator
                    below window sills
                on top of wch is an oak plank
                stained color of woodwork
            on which stand pots of plants
                    —one nice one—
                at each window
                    —new to me.

I hate to be a care & expense—
            but appreciate everything that is done for me
                and even now
            as Mary asked for a stamp
                said—
                "certainly—
                Take a lot—
                    Take two—"

I recall an article which I read years ago
                    upon the commandments,
                        the only one
                    with a promise of reward.
            Sometimes long life is a blessing
                    but—as always
            in human events—'circumstances alter cases'—
    as is clearly stated in Webster's spelling book.
My father's old age was an honor & a pleasure
                    while that of Aunt Eunice
                was an affliction to our family.
            Old age was a curse to her—

I long to see the sky—as
                    with white clouds overhead

                    White buildings—
    & snow outside is not interesting.

I think ¾ths of traffic has stopped—
                    on account of gas shortage.
        Mary sd she must cut down living expenses
                        still more.
    No deliveries as all young men are gone.
                Of course it is painful to me
                to have to be such an expense.
                    The Lord only knows
                whether I shall ever be of use
                        again.
    All sorts of animal life—bear pain. Thinking—

        goes on—regardless of time & place.
            Being will not die or fail.
The substitute nurse sat in my room
                    and had a fine rest
                    after raising 6 children
                    her husband is dead.
                It is the course of nature
                    to be dependent
                    at both ends of life.

A stiff southwest wind is playing
w/ the elms so that I feel in the woods.

I have not yet become adjusted to the movements
                              of the sun—
                                        Now—
if I put my head beside the window sill & look
                              straight up into the sky
it is almost as the line of top window sash
and will not get behind buildings
until I am in bed long after supper
& of course rises very late & is shining into
                              my west windows
until I am ready to go to sleep.

Our Lady of No Defense
blue light of the fields
of the farthest sea
release your care
    Stay loving
welfare or bad work
freeloader, & those gone mad
w/ desire, w/
    holes in thin shoes.
    Hold to yourself
to hell, ever

    loving children abide
Remember that love
even you could not make real
in each man / as in
the vision destroyed in yr eyes.

    Yr majesty
    to whom Curtis Mayfield & all men
    have talked at night
    Queen without a King

Or mother, lover, stranger
Seen going down the street
infant to adore, home to share
joy. Welcome the wanderer
        dignify the
broken heart & mind, nerves
& muscles.
Bless the south for the bums
And the leader of the birds flight
in the broken mind
wch is yr lord

When our need comes, feed us
from the life in closed eyes.
You are the preparer of the world.
My lady, my head is no hole, nor
                tender.
There are cats all over begging & stealing.
Don't leave me in cities & dripping tents.

I see a kerosene lamp moving across
the world at night. A flare led by a
sick child. The trees are a statue of all
future war, billowing w/ the indifference of
amassed rebirth in the mountain winds.

Why does it seem so lovely in the stars?
Because it takes so many years.
As the heart knows.

Blow us away from futility, folly
those bridges covered by
sea. Years.

Blow me, blow me into day
as a child or birds & blue sky, grace

Give me a mind
again

children's games
are still the same
tho the Baldwin apple
has changed

Richard Grossinger

Three Notes on Charles Olson

1.

The Sun in Olson is shining all the time, littering the plains with glacial rocks, following the rivers, inland, terminus to the sea. It is a generous sun, high in the sky. There is prana in the air. The River, neither Asian nor North American, is a planet river. The directions, as quadrants, are eternal.

The poet leaves us a map of the City. When he's gone, the same ruthless time that made him possible takes him calmly back into the Matrix.

The quarry sits, work of a titan, at all limits of the corporate space What he mashed into sand sears our gradient as boulders and talus slopes. He left us with a warning: those gods who made the arches and handles, who left their cuneiform copyright in gems, will return to their handiwork. They will sit in chairs of stone and scour the hills with rakes of water and ice.

Adhering to a more ancient final gnosticism. So that all of this reaches us through a ceremony, conducted at our deepest emotional center. Soundlessly, and without conventional wisdom.

The oneness of a cove a single rivulet reaches. Broken from the axis by current. He gathers that water in a bucket; he pours it back through the holes, burning zinc, Tyrian map/markings so precise of sky, they reappear in the membrane of the world.

So is Pisces smashed into limestone sandstone shale, she lies a fossil, a cone-bearer. Found in relics of an abandoned kingdom, as white and shining as she'll never be again.

O Troy, you perfect recall of the distances of stars. O stars who recall Troy to me in exactly the rain which is as close as you are far, hiding you in its clouds, without whom neither would exist—so does the rushing spirit end in whispers at my footsteps. O Troy, it was once a lightness, muthoi, we now know as darkness, because you are still here, because you are here and we have nothing left.

A ship stutters for a moment in the songs of sea fowl before the barrier veil, sails of African linen. The light falls across the mask and attracts the bearded stranger back into the stone.

He says, I will be a stranger among you, I who am so familiar.

Rocks. Stones. And above that, earth. Above that, air. Above that, light. And above that, night. And behind that, fire. The blue river in its bed. And below that, metal. A single stray material cloud in the air.

The energies, those that have not dissipated, remain to happen. Are happening.

Earth flat-out the galaxy.

Torso.

Mica.

Helen in the castle.

And beyond that, Asia, Cro Magnon. Flint.

And beyond that, chaos. Volcanoes. Thunderstorms. The attraction of flame to metal, the explosion outward, to the ocean's taut surface.

Grottoes dripping, hollow clay caves.

And beyond that, mind, intelligence.

And beyond that, fish.

The single taproot, fibrous. Coming apart coming together.

The Egyptian palm. The glyph for wheat. The waxing moon. The stalk for wind. The cessation of wind.

The Chinese emperor sits at a gate in the stars.

The geometry is broken along the Caucasus.

Planet — and beyond its blue skies, where sun fills history, as Charles saw in Gloucester — is unabating eternal refilling night. And within night, mind.

The boats forming on the seesaw tide.

Lichen. Seeds. The eagle. The hooded rider.

The rounded mountains of the East. Champlain's vessels.

Yarn. The eye that nails them to turbulence.

And within that, turquoise.

Within the atomic sheathes, the wheat gripped by the stewards, the ridges. The rivets. The river carrying water to the end of flow.

Within that, I sit, containing all as petals, at my boundaries, define me, and cease.

3.

Singleness is a primitive condition.

BOOK OF THE CRANBERRY ISLANDS

BY RICHARD GROSSINGER

"Against the weight and tension of circumstances of Mount Desert Island" where he spent eight months doing ethnographic fieldwork on Maine lobster fishing, Richard Grossinger created this original and poetic work.

"Book of the Cranberry Islands, as a narrative of mixed prose forms, is difficult to categorize because it borrows from so many different genres without becoming fully any one of them. Depending on one's preference, the book is either a novel, an ethnography, a philosophical journal, or a long regional poem in the William Carlos Williams − Charles Olson tradition. I experience the form not as a hybrid but as my own, and I assume that radical art means simply that the artist always makes his own (as well as content) form... . . .

"Book of the Cranberry Islands is a statement of a level of being. That level comes into being as the book does, grows with it, changes gradually as its energies are transformed into other orders of energy, and ultimately passes through itself into a totally other thing. The book itself is the discovery, the journey." − *from the book*

A Harper Colophon Book   CN/373 $5.95

Harper & Row
Paperback Dept.
10 E. 53d St., New York 10022

THE NEW WORLD WRITING

NORTHERN MISTS by Carl O. Sauer

The New World's finest historical geographer reconstructs the early Irish, Viking & Portuguese voyages into the North Atlantic. "Sauer loves the language, gently, without exploitation, and the deliberate flow of words is a delight. Fundamentally, however, it is his depths that hold us" — Paul Metcalf. Paperback edition, $3.50. 204 pp. Dozens of maps.

RECOLLECTIONS OF GRAN APACHERIA by Edward Dorn

The author of *Gunslinger* on the destruction of the Apache nation, a brilliant, bitter yet lyrical, text. "Gran Apacheria is a powerful work, worthy of great praise, and deserving of high stature in our literature" — Poetry Flash. Newsprint edition, $2.00. Letter-press hardcover, $12.00. 48 pages, Illustrated by Michael Myers.

SHABOGEK by Jaime de Angulo

A first volume sequel to the author's classic *Indian Tales* .... The Bear party, many years later, spend the winter at Clear Lake, weaving baskets & telling tales. "Jaime de Angulo is the American Ovid" — Ezra Pound. "One of the most outstanding writers I have ever encountered" — William C. Williams. Letter-press hardcover, $12.00. 104 pp. Available Oct. 1, 1976.

SPEARMINT & ROSEMARY by Charles Olson

A previously unpublished variation on the author's famous Maximus cycle, not included in the larger collections. "Olson is the Great Fire Source; we all return to him time & time again" — Robert Duncan. Chapbook, $2.00. 16 pages.

MAN IN NATURE by Carl O. Sauer

A children's introduction to the cultural regions of the New World, and the Indian peoples who occupied these regions on the eve of European colonization. A fundamental reference text for the study of New World Cultures. Paperback edition, $7.95. Hardcover edition, $15.00. Hundreds of illustrations.

Direct orders, and address inquiries:

Turtle Island Foundation
2845 Buena Vista Way
Berkeley, California 94708

THE LANDSCAPE PAPERS by Edgar Anderson

This text contains all of the essays Anderson contributed, post *Plants, Man & Life*, to *Landscape* Magazine, founded and then edited in the Souwest by J.B. Jackson. Paperback edition, $4.00. Hardcover, $10.00. Available, Oct. 1, 1976.

APALACHE by Paul Metcalf

Based solely on historical documents from the greater Appalachian region, Metcalf's Apalache becomes an extraordinarily powerful and moving symphonic poem of the American experience. "The central intellectual conflict today is between those who are attempting to reconstruct American history along multi-cultural lines, and those who wish it to remain a rude center of colonial provincialism. APALACHE is on the winning side" — Ishmael Reed. "The book of this or any other year" — Sand Dollar Newsletter. Letter-press hardcover, $12.00. 196 pages.

IDOLS by Bob Callahan

A New World poem by the editor of the Turtle Island publications series. "Callahan's interests are clearly multi-cultural. His work should be compared, equally, to the lyrics of the classic blues, the songs of the Ghost Dance religion, as well as to the documents and writings of the first white settlers" — Daily Californian. Letter-press chapbook, $3.00.

HOW THE WORLD WAS MADE by Jaime de Angulo

The second volume in the author's sequel to *Indian Tales*. In this text, the ancient priest, Old Man Turtle, takes the young wolf/man, Tsimmu, on a tour of the religious ceremonies being held at Clear Lake during the first week of Spring. Letter-press hardcover, $12.00. Available, Oct. 1, 1976.

NEW WORLD JOURNAL #1 ed. by Bob Callahan

The first issue of this now ongoing review contains essays & poems by Pomo historian William, Bob Callahan, botanist Edgar Anderson, ethnologist & poet Robert Barlow, poet Ernesto Cardenal, geographer Carl Sauer, and poet Charles Olson. "A wonderful generation of geographers, poets, botanists, and linguists who took the risk of grounding their work in the literal historical landscape of the West" — San Francisco Review of Books. Letter-press paper edition, $3.00.

Direct orders, and address inquiries to:

Turtle Island Foundation
2845 Buena Vista Way
Berkeley, California 94708

The Cranberry Island Sequence by Richard Grossinger (six books)
$5.00 each, or $18.00 for the set

Book of the Cranberry Islands (1969) (Harper and Row edition, regularly $5.95)
The Provinces (1970)
The Long Body of the Dream (1971)
The Book of Being Born Again into the World (1972)
The Windy Passage from Nostalgia (1973)
The Slag of Creation (1974)

The All-American Revival Church Sequence (essays) by Richard Grossinger

Early Field-Notes from the All-American Revival Church (1972)
   (Io Edition—$3.50)
Martian Homecoming at the All-American Revival Church (1974)—$3.00.
The Unfinished Business of Doctor Hermes (1976)—$4.00.
The Set: $7.50.

Mars: A Science Fiction Vision by Richard Grossinger (Io Edition—$3.50)

All ten books by Richard Grossinger: $26.00.

Changing Woman by Lindy Hough (Io Edition—$2.00).
Psyche by Lindy Hough—$3.00.
The Sun in Cancer by Lindy Hough—$3.50.

Three books by Lindy Hough: $5.00.

A Kansas Cycle by Paul Kahn—$2.50.
Deutschland and Other Places by Josephine Clare—$3.00.
Poems and Glyphs by Charles Stein (Io Edition—$2.50).
Love Minus Zero by Frank Zero (Io Edition—$2.00).
Selected Poems, 1956-1975 by Diane di Prima—$5.00.
Synthesis by Theodore Enslin—$6.00.
The Year Book by Alex Gildzen—$3.00.
Here by Bobby Byrd—$3.00.
The Girl with the Stone in Her Lap by Irene McKinny—$4.00.
Aesop's Garden by Don Byrd—$4.00.
20,000 A.D. by Edward Sanders—$3,50.
Memory by Bernadette Mayer—$3.50.
Sand Cast by Wayne Turiansky—$2.00.
The Heavenly Tree Grows Downward by Gerrit Lansing (forthcoming)—$4.00.
Fan Poems by Tom Clark—$3.00.
Spring and Autumn Annals by Diane di Prima (forthcoming)—$6.00.

By Subscription: $9.00 per three books (as they appear).

A Full Set of Io through #21: $81.50, through #23: $89.50.
Io Subscription: #12.00 per four issues.

The Figures announces publication of an

EXHIBITION CATALOG OF 1970'S ALL STARS

BASEBALL
by
Tom Clark

80 pp., 7x10, BASEBALL features
32 paintings, eleven in full color, and each
with an accompanying text spoken by the portrait itself.

Available in the trade edition at $6.50,
or in a special numbered and signed edition limited to
50 copies, each with a color photograph tipped in, at $15.

Order from:
Serendipity Books Distribution
1790 Shattuck Ave.
Berkeley, CA 94709

GODDARD COLLEGE

GODDARD COLLEGE MASTER'S DEGREE PROGRAMS for self-directed adults. Studies designed with help of faculty advisor to meet individual needs. Seminars on the Vermont campus, or at Goddard Graduate Program centers in six major cities. A wide range of faculty resources and a varied student body. Enrollment continuous throughout the year; several study options; non-discriminatory admissions.

Write: Graduate Program Admissions, Box I, Goddard College, Plainfield, Vermont 05667.

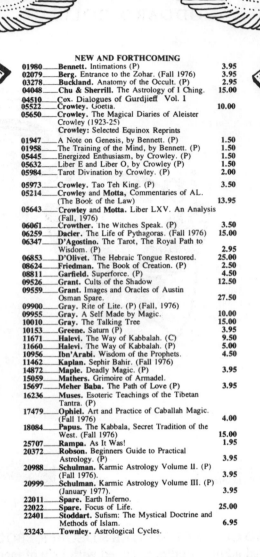

NEW AND FORTHCOMING

01980	**Bennett.** Intimations (P)	3.95
02079	**Berg.** Entrance to the Zohar. (Fall 1976)	3.95
03278	**Buckland.** Anatomy of the Occult. (P)	2.95
04048	**Chu & Sherrill.** The Astrology of I Ching.	15.00
04510	**Cox.** Dialogues of Gurdjieff Vol. 1	
05522	**Crowley.** Goetia.	10.00
05650	**Crowley.** The Magical Diaries of Aleister Crowley (1923-25)	

Crowley: Selected Equinox Reprints

01947	A Note on Genesis, by Bennett. (P)	1.50
01958	The Training of the Mind, by Bennett. (P)	1.50
05445	Energized Enthusiasm, by Crowley. (P)	1.50
05632	Liber E and Liber O, by Crowley (P)	1.50
05984	Tarot Divination by Crowley. (P)	2.00
05973	**Crowley.** Tao Teh King. (P)	3.50
05214	**Crowley and Motta,** Commentaries of AL. (The Book of the Law)	13.95
05643	**Crowley and Motta.** Liber LXV. An Analysis (Fall, 1976)	
06061	**Crowther.** The Witches Speak. (P)	3.50
06259	**Dacier.** The Life of Pythagoras. (Fall 1976)	15.00
06347	**D'Agostino.** The Tarot, The Royal Path to Wisdom. (P)	2.95
06853	**D'Olivet.** The Hebraic Tongue Restored.	25.00
08624	**Friedman.** The Book of Creation. (P)	2.50
08811	**Garfield.** Superforce. (P)	4.50
09526	**Grant.** Cults of the Shadow	12.50
09559	**Grant.** Images and Oracles of Austin Osman Spare.	27.50
09900	**Gray.** Rite of Lite. (P) (Fall, 1976)	
09955	**Gray.** A Self Made by Magic.	10.00
10010	**Gray.** The Talking Tree	15.00
10153	**Greene.** Saturn (P)	3.95
11671	**Halevi.** The Way of Kabbalah. (C)	9.50
11660	**Halevi.** The Way of Kabbalah. (P)	5.00
10956	**Ibn'Arabi.** Wisdom of the Prophets.	4.50
11462	**Kaplan.** Sephir Bahir. (Fall 1976)	
14872	**Maple.** Deadly Magic. (P)	3.95
15059	**Mathers.** Grimoire of Armadel.	
15697	**Meher Baba.** The Path of Love (P)	3.95
16236	**Muses.** Esoteric Teachings of the Tibetan Tantra. (P)	
17479	**Ophiel.** Art and Practice of Caballah Magic. (Fall 1976)	4.00
18084	**Papus.** The Kabbala, Secret Tradition of the West. (Fall 1976)	15.00
25707	**Rampa.** As It Was!	1.95
20372	**Robson.** Beginners Guide to Practical Astrology. (P)	3.95
20988	**Schulman.** Karmic Astrology Volume II. (P) (Fall 1976).	3.95
20999	**Schulman.** Karmic Astrology Volume III. (P) (January 1977).	3.95
22011	**Spare.** Earth Inferno.	
22022	**Spare.** Focus of Life.	25.00
22401	**Stoddart.** Sufism: The Mystical Doctrine and Methods of Islam.	6.95
23243	**Townley.** Astrological Cycles.	

SAMUEL WEISER

INC.

625 Broadway
New York, New York 10012

Specialists in Occult and Oriental Philosophy